Changed

Alive Publishing

Changed

stories of God's power to change lives

by
Tara
HOLMES

First published in 2005 by Alive Publishing Ltd,
Graphic House, 124 City Road, Stoke on Trent ST4 2PH
Tel: +44 (0) 1782 745600 Fax: +44 (0) 1782 745500
www.biblealive.co.uk   e-mail:editor@biblealive.co.uk

© 2005 Tara Holmes
British Library Catalogue-in-Publication Data. A catalogue record for
this book is available from the British Library.

ISBN: 0-9540335-7-4

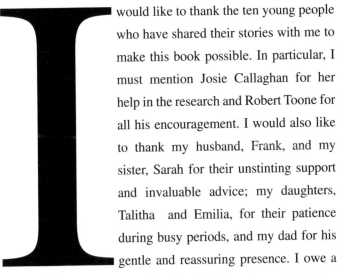would like to thank the ten young people who have shared their stories with me to make this book possible. In particular, I must mention Josie Callaghan for her help in the research and Robert Toone for all his encouragement. I would also like to thank my husband, Frank, and my sister, Sarah for their unstinting support and invaluable advice; my daughters, Talitha and Emilia, for their patience during busy periods, and my dad for his gentle and reassuring presence. I owe a debt of gratitude to my friend and fellow journalist, Bess Twiston Davies, and Mike and Sue Conway and all at *Alive Publishing* for their time and energy in bringing this book to fruition. I must also thank my longtime friend Paula Stringer for all her prayers and inspiration.

About the author

Tara Holmes is a freelance journalist who began her career at the age of 16, combining part-time work on local newspapers in Birmingham with her A level and university studies. After graduating with distinction from journalism college in 1994, she was given an award by the French media group, Bayard Presse, for her contribution to print journalism. She moved to Manchester and worked as a journalist on *The Universe* Catholic weekly for two years. In 1996, aged 25, she was appointed deputy editor of the *Catholic Times*. She left the post in 2001 to pursue a career as a freelance journalist, and is now a regular contributor to *The Times*. She has published articles in *The Irish Post, Good Health* and *Black Hair* magazines. She also writes for the Paris-based magazine *Today* and continues to work for Catholic publications including *Bible Alive, Catholic World Report, Catholic Today* and *Lourdes Magazine*.

Tara is married with two young children and lives in Cheshire.

Contents

Dedication

In memory of my mum, whose love and faith continues to inspire my spiritual journey.

Foreword

by Bishop Arthur Roche

Reading this book was like a baptismal experience for me. At times I felt that I was descending into the waters of modern-day life with all its horror stories, broken relationships, drug abuse, and abortions. Then, when the witnesses described their moments of personal conversion, I felt, through the vividness and candour of their testimonies, that I was rising with them to that new life which Christ has made available to us all.

The ten stories contained within these covers are without exception fascinating. How can they not be, since they each describe something extraordinary: the inrushing of God's Holy Spirit into the lives of young men and women of our own time? These are stories about love, about the ultimately inexpressible joy of knowing that God loves us more than we are capable of imagining.

As a result of reading this book, I feel, as a bishop, newly capable of understanding young people's difficulties with faith. It is heartbreaking to read about their quiet desperation as they search for a meaning in their lives without having anybody to provide them with a moral compass. Should we be surprised if they succumb to the prevailing climate of self-gratification? What else is there, when one has scarcely begun one's life and yet cannot discover any reason for hope?

I also feel that these young people have evangelised me. They have reminded me of God's power to change people's lives, often at times when the darkness seemed most intense. In these pages we read of young people's first experiences of prayer. We see a young man, whose alcoholic mother has returned home drunk again and lies in the hallway beside him, seriously injured by broken glass, fingering rosary beads for the first time as he awaits the arrival of the ambulance.

As I have reflected on such powerful images, another image comes to my mind, this time from scripture. It is from the Book of Wisdom: 'as sparks run through the stubble, so will they' (3:7). These are enigmatic lines and they are often heard at funerals. For me, they capture two important truths about young people today. Firstly, they convey the emotions of parents, who see their beloved sons and daughters dissipating their energies foolishly and unwholesomely, so that their lives flare but lack direction; and beneath all the show, ashes lie smouldering. Secondly, they speak deeply and mysteriously about life: the stubble must be burnt away if these same young men and women are to experience that new growth which comes in God's good time.

The Right Reverend Arthur Roche
Bishop of Leeds
The Solemnity of Mary, Mother of God, 1 January 2005.

Introduction

It was during a conversation with Robert Toone, national director of Youth 2000, that the idea for *Changed* first came to mind. Robert had spoken movingly of the numerous young people whose lives had been transformed through Youth 2000. Many of them had powerful stories of conversion. Some had previously attempted suicide. Others had been involved in crime, football violence, drugs and alcohol abuse. Yet they had all found fresh hope and courage through meeting other young people on fire with God's love. Robert and I agreed that a book which featured some of these stories would be a powerful tool in the Church's work of evangelisation. *Changed* is the culmination of that idea. It tells the stories of ten young people from all walks of life who have been touched by Youth 2000 and witnessed to God's grace in the most extraordinary ways. It features married couples with families, single people and those who have found a vocation to religious life or the priesthood. Some testimonies are dramatic stories of conversion. Others testify to God's hand at work during difficult times – sexual abuse, depression, family breakdown and the loss of loved ones. Three of the stories are linked to pilgrimages to Medjugorje in the former Yugoslavia, where it is claimed that the Virgin Mary appears. Like Catholics throughout the world, young people involved with Youth 2000 who have had conversion experiences in Medjugorje are awaiting the Church's final judgement on the events there.

In coming forward, all of the young people have made themselves vulnerable for the sake of God's kingdom. In *Changed*, they share intimate details of their lives, warts and all, in the hope that you, the reader, may journey into a deeper relationship with Our Lord and Saviour, Jesus Christ. In taking such a risk, they have for the first time given Youth 2000 a unique opportunity to reach beyond the confines of a retreat or a prayer group to people everywhere.

Through Youth 2000 many young people have stood up at retreats and given their testimony. Because they have shared their faith journey in this way, thousands of others have been inspired to seek forgiveness and healing. For many young people, a retreat has been a turning point, enabling them to receive the gospel afresh through the action of the Holy Spirit. For others it has been their first encounter with Jesus Christ and his Church.

Youth 2000 was founded in 1990 by Ernest Williams. It was set up in response to Pope John Paul II's call to young people to be 'witnesses of faith and love' at World Youth Day in Santiago de Compostela in 1989. Ernest, then aged 26, had been amongst thousands of young people present. Immediately after World Youth Day, he went on pilgrimage to Fatima. During a period of prayer and reflection in front of the Blessed Sacrament, an image came to him of a chain of young people around the world in Eucharistic adoration. This vision led Ernest to found Youth 2000, a new initiative that would draw young people closer to the heart of Jesus through the Mass, adoration of the Blessed Sacrament, reading the Bible, Confession and devotion to Mary, the Mother of God.

Since then Youth 2000 has spread to 24 countries worldwide and been the catalyst for countless conversion experiences. Each August the annual prayer festival in Walsingham attracts over 1500 young people. It is the largest residential event for Catholic youth in Britain and has played a massive role in bringing young people back to the Church.

In October 2003 Pope John Paul II praised Youth 2000's work in his address to the bishops of England and Wales in Rome. The organisation has received widespread support from the English and Welsh bishops, including Cardinal Cormac Murphy-O'Connor and Archbishop Vincent Nichols of Birmingham. Bishop Thomas McMahon of Brentwood and Bishop Arthur Roche of Leeds are patrons of Youth 2000. I first became involved with Youth 2000 in 1990, at the age of 19. As a student I regularly attended retreats, particularly in the early years, when we would sleep on the floor and then get up in the night to pray in front of the Blessed Sacrament. I also met my husband for the first time on a retreat at Woldingham School in Surrey in 1993.

By hearing the stories of the ten young people who feature in this book, I have been challenged to seek healing in areas of my own life. I hope that you too may be touched by the testimonies of these young people who have put themselves on the line to glorify God. Many of them have spoken to me about how sharing their story has helped them in their own healing process. I hope that their experiences will enable you, the reader, to put your own difficulties and struggles into perspective and open the gates for a special time of grace in your life.

We are all sinners. We all have our weaknesses, difficulties, joys and sorrows. But we can all learn from each other as we seek to embrace Christ more fully in our lives.

Tara Holmes,
The Immaculate Conception of the Blessed Virgin Mary,
8th December 2004

Chapter 1
Brother Francis

CHANGED LIFE

1. **NAME:** Brother Francis, formerly Troy Edkins
2. **DATE OF BIRTH:** February 13th 1971
3. **PLACE OF BIRTH:** Ilford, Essex
4. **FAMILY:** Youngest of 2 sons, parents divorced
5. **EDUCATION:** A truant from Loxford Secondary School
6. **TEENAGE AMBITION:** To be a builder
7. **CURRENT OCCUPATION:** A radical Franciscan friar for life
8. **TURNING POINT:** Finding a picture of Jesus in a telephone box

Brother Francis

Standing alone in a telephone box, Troy Edkins slammed down the receiver and reached deep into his pocket for a bottle of pills. He frantically tore off the lid and tipped the pills into his hand. He opened his mouth and swallowed them one by one. Then he panicked. He flung open the door of the phone box, stumbled out and dragged himself in the direction of the nearest hospital. His heart was pounding so hard it felt as if it would burst through his chest. Terrified, he staggered into the hospital, screaming for help. He collapsed in a heap on the floor. Two minutes later and he would have been dead.

Troy was on the verge of a coma when the doctors hauled him into theatre and pumped his stomach. He woke to find his family at his bedside. At first he was ashamed and angry for having tried to take his own life. Then he began to realize how lucky he had been to survive.

During his time in hospital, Troy's mind returned to the events leading up to his suicide attempt. He had just had an argument with his girlfriend of two years. After a desperate conversation with her on the phone, he had finally tipped over the edge. The writing had been on the wall for some time, but Troy still couldn't accept the relationship was all but over. Life at home was equally distressing. His mum was an alcoholic, a constant stream of her drinking partners were staying at the house and he was really missing his dad.

Troy's dad had left home when he was two, and his mum had struggled to bring up him and his older brother, Paul. 'It was really stressful for my mum because she really loved my dad', he says, sadly. 'At Christmas my mum would find it particularly hard being on her own but she would still give us the best presents. We were everything to her. She really tried to give us the best in life.'

His mum turned to drink when he was about seven years old. Some of her boyfriends moved in, but this caused constant tension and arguments. Growing up without his father at home, Troy had always felt an 'emptiness'. During his early teens, Troy would meet his dad at a sleazy strip club called *The Kings*. His dad, a guitarist in a rock band, worked there as a DJ. 'It was a boxing club and a strip joint', he explains. 'The lads would box and then a stripper would come into the ring'.

At home with his mum, Troy's life also knew few moral boundaries. He started stealing at the age of six. One of his earliest memories is of stealing from a guest during a party at his house. 'He must have been drunk', he recalls. 'I nicked his St Christopher medal. When he woke up he had a cup of tea and off he went, none the wiser. I would wear it to school under my uniform.'

Another time, after the family had moved to Southend-on-Sea in Essex, he stole a box of fish from a fishmonger's. 'I went home and put it straight into the freezer', he recalls. He also once stole a pile of magazines from a newsagent at 6 a.m. and then sold them to old ladies on the street. He would regularly steal sweets and cigarettes. 'I used to steal from an old lady', he recalls. 'The bell would go off when you entered the shop and she would take a while to reach the counter. In the meantime, I'd stuff my pockets with sweets and cigarettes. I also nicked my clothes, records and CDs. It was to do with greed and selfishness. My mum would bend over backwards to give me the latest gear, but I became more and more materialistic. I would abuse her goodwill and take it for granted. If there was a pair of trainers in fashion, I'd beg her to get them for me. She would give in even though she couldn't afford them.'

At school, he never worked. He didn't turn up for most of his exams. Those he did sit he failed. One weekend he broke into his school, turned the taps on full blast and flooded his classroom. After that he was too scared to go back and began to play truant. As a teenager Troy experimented with solvent abuse, particularly butane gas. In his late teens he used poppers to get high and remembers turning blue from the effect. He was also a heavy smoker.

He was introduced to ouija boards by a school friend and took part in seances from the age of 14. He also tried reading tarot cards. 'At the time it didn't scare me', he reveals. 'I just thought it was weird. But it did make me question if there was such a thing as the devil.'

His curiosity was overtaken by more immediate concerns. He became interested in girls and started to experiment with sex. By now, he was six foot eight inches tall and good looking. There was an endless supply of girlfriends and young women desperate to win his affection. He met most of his girlfriends in nightclubs. When he became serious with a girl, he would have her name tattooed on his arm. 'I did sometimes say I was in love', he reveals. 'But looking back I realize it was immaturity and lust'.

He lurched from one relationship to another without knowing any real happiness. His first serious girlfriend lasted four months. The next two relationships both lasted a year. One of his girlfriends became pregnant with his baby. Both he and his mum begged the girl to keep the child. Troy was devastated when she decided to press ahead with an abortion.

It was against this backdrop that he became involved with Joanne, the young woman who was part of the reason he tried to commit suicide. Troy was seventeen when he met Joanne. She worked as a waitress in a nightclub in Dagenham. An intense relationship soon developed. 'We became more and more dependent on each other',Troy recalls.'It was psychologically damaging. There was a lot of jealousy on both sides. The tables would turn constantly and each of us would gloat if the other was jealous. We would try to gain the other's adoration and ended up virtually worshipping each other. It was crazy.' Disillusioned, he stood in a field near his home one night, looked at the sky and cried out at the top of his voice: 'God, if you are really there, prove it to me'.

Convinced that his cry for help had fallen on deaf ears, Troy went back to square one. He and Joanne would constantly cheat on each other. Things came to a head when Troy discovered Joanne was having an affair. Eaten up with jealousy, he decided to teach his girlfriend's lover a lesson he wouldn't forget. Troy stormed into the shop where the young man was working and hit him across the face. When he fell to the ground under the weight of the blow, Troy marched out. As far as Troy was concerned, the incident had the desired effect: the man never approached Joanne again. From now on no other man would touch his girl. Troy started to imagine a future with Joanne. 'For a while I thought everything was great and we'd get married'. Fresh problems emerged when he began a new job as a double-glazing salesman. 'The turnover of staff was incredible', he says. 'Most of the girls had bad reputations and most of the guys, including myself, were idiots. It was one big ego trip.'

As the novelty of the new job wore off, Troy began to detest his work. His relationship with Joanne was on the rocks. The more Troy lost his hold on Joanne, who had complex personal problems of her own, the more obsessed he became with her.

On a summer's night in 1991, Troy decided to make a last-ditch attempt to patch up his relationship with Joanne. Before he left the house he snatched a bottle of his mum's anti-depressants and stuffed it into his trouser pocket. He decided to go and call Joanne from a phone box. If everything went well, fine. But if things went wrong there were always the pills. He took a deep breath as Joanne answered the phone. The rest of the conversation was a blur of screaming and shouting. Troy was shaking with anger. This time he knew he had lost her. If he went home, he would face the depressing scene of his mum's drinking partners. Suicide seemed to be the only option.

Burdened with guilt, Joanne came to visit him in hospital. 'We tried to get back together but I was emotionally blackmailing her', he says. Troy finally accepted that the situation was hopeless, and he and Joanne went their separate ways. After being discharged from hospital his outlook on life became increasingly dark. 'I moved twelve times in a year', he recalls. 'I would stay at a friend's, go back to my mum's, move in with a girlfriend, get a place of my own, move in with a girlfriend...' At one point, he shared a flat with six friends. All of them were criminals and most of them took drugs. 'We did a burglary at a shop at 3 a.m. one Friday night and got caught', he says. 'We brought some of the stuff to the flat, and then six policemen broke in and arrested us'.

Unlikely as it might seem, the arrest marked a turning point in Troy's life. He and the others were taken to the police station and detained overnight. Troy was released the following morning, and no charges were brought against him as it was his first major offence. His companions, who were all known to the police, were kept in custody and eventually sent down. Struck by his lucky escape, Troy returned to the flat in Ilford. The landlord, presuming Troy had been charged for the burglary along with the others, had no idea he was there. Troy was effectively living in a squat.

He was also desperate to find a new direction in his life. He stole a book on philosophy from his local library and approached his friend's father, who was a spiritual healer, with his questions. But he didn't get the answers he was looking for. He took up T'ai Chi, an ancient Chinese form of classical dance for health and self-development, which he would practise in a forest. 'But it didn't have any meaning, it was shallow', he says.

He abandoned T'ai Chi but his quest for the truth continued. A few weeks later, he found a picture of Jesus, the Divine Mercy, inside a phone box. Beneath the gentle image were the words 'Jesus, I trust in you'. 'I started wondering: "Who is Jesus Christ?" I couldn't remember anything from school except that he was born in Bethlehem and nailed to the cross. In fact, I thought his head was nailed as well.'

He visited a Catholic bookshop in Ilford and chatted to the lady behind the counter. To his amazement, she gave him a picture of the Divine Mercy, the exact same image of Christ that he had found in the phone box. The woman also gave him a copy of the Gospel of John. He was overwhelmed when he opened the Gospel and read the opening lines: 'In the beginning was the Word: the Word was with God and the Word was God...The Word was the real light that gives light to everyone...and the world did not recognise him' (John 1:1, 9-10). As he read the last line, Troy was struck by the image of Jesus as the light not recognized by the world. 'That was the instant I knew that Jesus was God', he reveals. That was also the moment he converted to Christianity.

In the months that followed, Troy would often return to the bookshop. Standing among the spiritual books, statues and crucifixes, he felt a great sense of peace. He was on the dole at the time and would spend his entire giro on books from the shop. The woman who had given him the Divine Mercy prayer card he now knew as Kathy Goble. She would patiently answer all his questions. 'All my life, I felt like I'd been walking around with an empty glass trying to find some water and no one had anything to give me. Then suddenly I'd walked into a fountain.' A whole new world had opened up, and with it came a whole new vocabulary. 'Eucharist, tabernacle and genuflect', he says. 'These were all new words for me. I was bursting with excitement, knowing I'd found the truth. I was on cloud nine.'

Not long afterwards, Troy decided he would like to go to church. It was March 1992, and he hadn't been inside a church since being baptized into the Church of England as a baby. Ironically, the church he chose to attend was opposite the strip club he used to frequent as a teenager. On his first visit a priest was leading the stations of the cross. 'The first thing I thought when I saw the priest was: "I want to do that". I'd been reading a book on the life of St Francis of Assisi. I'd been blown away by how he had emptied himself and had passionately lived the life of Christ in such a radical way. In a vision, Jesus said to St Francis from the cross: "Go and rebuild my church. It's falling down." I wanted to be like him.'

In the meantime, Kathy from the bookshop had paid for him to attend a Youth 2000 retreat at the Sion Community house in Brentwood. The retreat, held on the Palm Sunday weekend, was packed full of young people. Father John Armitage, spiritual director to Youth 2000, gave a talk on confession. Later Troy, desperate to confess his sins, approached the priest in the confessional. As a non-Catholic, Troy was not able to make a full confession. 'Father John explained to me that he couldn't give me absolution. I didn't know what that was anyway.' The priest, however, did give Troy some sound advice which he still remembers to this day. 'Even without absolution, I felt the healing process had started. On a human level I could see that it's good for us to confess our sins.' At the end of the retreat Troy stood up and spoke about the need for young people to pray outside abortion clinics. By now he had realized that life was a gift. Even one which had been as desperate as his own could be transformed by faith in Jesus Christ. Still deeply affected by the loss of the child he had fathered during his teenage years, Troy was trembling with fear. It was the first time he had ever spoken in public.

At home, life with his mum was still difficult. After the Youth 2000 retreat, Troy carried on with his practice of spiritual reading. Late one night he was reading a book about Mary when he heard a voice in his head, saying: 'Pray for your mum'. At first he ignored it because he was so engrossed in the book. But the voice grew louder and more urgent. After he heard it a third time, he felt alarmed and began to pray. Three minutes later, his mum arrived home from the pub, carrying a pint glass. She staggered through the door, falling onto the glass, which smashed into her face. 'She lay in a pool of blood', says Troy. 'I called an ambulance, got down on my knees and prayed my first rosary. The ambulance arrived about twenty minutes later, just as I got to the end of the rosary.'

At the hospital doctors told Troy that his mum had narrowly missed rupturing her jugular vein when she collapsed on to the glass. For him, the near miss was a testimony to the power of prayer.

In the following year 1993, Troy was received into the Catholic Church. He faced his first major test as a Catholic when he celebrated his twenty-third birthday in February 1994. His uncle took him to a nightclub where he got chatting to an old friend. At first he talked to her about his faith. But after several drinks the conversation hit a downward spiral, and he ended up spending the night with her. The following morning, desperate to bring God into the situation despite the disastrous turn of events, he left a prayer card and a medal in the girl's flat. As he walked out into the daylight, his head was swimming. 'I had my rosary around my neck but I had still ended up denying Christ despite my experience of conversion', he says. 'I felt like I'd rejected Christ and abandoned all the blessings I'd been given. It was as if I'd chucked them back into his face. Yet, despite what I'd done, I knew Jesus was everything. I still wanted to evangelize.'

Overcome with remorse, Troy went straight to confession. 'I was overwhelmed by the forgiveness and mercy of Christ through the grace of confession. I was learning the path of virtue and the importance of denying myself. God was leading me slowly and I was being weaned off my past sicknesses. I felt a new surge of life and wanted to keep living for Jesus.' The experience marked another turning-point. Realizing that he needed the support of a community to live the Christian life, Troy decided to leave Essex. He headed up to Craig Lodge, a retreat centre in Dalmally, Scotland. It was on a Youth 2000 retreat there, that he first felt the call to community life.

Troy was now ready to test that call. After a successful two-week trial period, he officially joined the Krisevac

Community at Craig Lodge on 13 May 1994, the feast of Our Lady of Fatima. During his time there, Troy faced the challenges of community living. He struggled to give up smoking and would hide his cigarettes behind an icon of Mary in the chapel. He felt increasingly drawn to the Franciscan Friars of the Renewal, a radical religious order living in the Bronx, a notoriously tough district of New York. Troy had met one of the friars, Father Stan Fortuna, at a Youth 2000 retreat the previous summer. Father Stan was a rapper and talented musician whose songs and inspiring talks to young people had made an impression on him.

'Seeing him in his sandals, and simple patched grey habit and hearing him speak from the heart made me want to join'. Troy also felt called to the order because of his new devotion to the Eucharist and Mary, which had been bolstered by his experience with Youth 2000.

Troy's vocation to the friars was confirmed at the end of 1994, at the tomb of St Francis during a trip to Assisi. The saint's habit was amongst the relics on display in the basilica there. 'I saw his habit was grey and felt a strong desire to wear the Franciscan habit, live in a cell and have a beard', he laughs.

The following May, Troy visited the friars in the Bronx. Initially, the superior, Father Glenn Sudano, was reluctant to let him join. 'The friars had not had any vocations from overseas: there were only twenty-five brothers at the time and they were all American. Father Glenn mentioned a community in Italy. He also suggested that I could move to New York and work with Youth 2000 there. But I said I felt called to start living with the brothers that September.' Troy's total belief in his vocation to the New York friars convinced the community to give him a chance on the condition that he gave up smoking. He pledged never to smoke again. To this day he has not smoked another cigarette.

For the first six months in the Bronx, Troy was a postulant. Dressed in a white shirt and grey trousers, he lived the life of a brother while he discerned his vocation. At the end of the period of discernment, he became a novice, taking the same name he had chosen for his confirmation – Francis. From that moment on, he became known as Brother Francis. At Easter 1997 he took his first vows of poverty, chastity and obedience. It was a time of great joy because back in London his brother Paul, now married with five children, had decided to become a Catholic and was received into the Church.

For the next five years, Brother Francis lived in the Bronx, working with the homeless in a neighbourhood with a multitude of problems including drug and alcohol abuse, under-age pregnancies and gang rivalry. He took his final vows on 29 July 2000. As he lay prostrate during the litany of the saints his joy was indescribable. He also met Blessed Mother Teresa in the Bronx, who told him to 'do everything for Jesus through Mary'. And, with the encouragement of his superior, he discovered he was a gifted artist and took classes. He has since painted portraits of the Pope and Mother Teresa and set up an Internet gallery (www.Godsgallery.org.uk) to inspire young artists to develop their talents.

In 2002 he moved back to England from New York. The Franciscan Friars of the Renewal had set up a friary in Canning Town, East London, in 2000. Brother Francis joined the five-strong community there, only fifteen minutes away from his home town, where his mum has recently taken enormous steps to overcome her alcohol addiction. The friars live an intense life of prayer, run a soup kitchen for the homeless and pray outside abortion clinics. They also have a strong presence at Youth 2000 retreats and prayer groups in London.

The desire to help young people find Jesus is close to Brother Francis' heart. He feels a particular affinity to those who have been through similar experiences to himself. To those who find chastity difficult, he points to his own past struggles and the importance of fidelity to Christ. 'Jesus was chaste and he's our ideal. I've always loved the lives of the saints. The majority of the saints were priests and religious who led a chaste, celibate life. We're all called to imitate the saints. Married couples, too, are called to a life of chastity, by saying "yes" to one man or woman for the rest of their lives.' To those who have attempted suicide and are struggling with feelings of self-hatred, Brother Francis points to the healing love of Jesus Christ through Eucharistic adoration and praying the rosary. In the same way that Youth 2000 prepared the way for his life as a brother, he believes that all young people, no matter how bad their situation, can also come to know Christ as their Saviour.

'To quote St Augustine: "Our hearts are restless until they rest in him". I always wanted to rest my heart somewhere but I didn't know where. I stumbled across God and I fell at his feet. Surviving the suicide attempt made me realize he had a bigger plan for me. God was preparing me for the work I do now.'

Chapter 2

Natalie Ritchie

CHANGED LIFE

1. **NAME:** Natalie Ritchie
2. **DATE OF BIRTH:** June 26th 1983
3. **PLACE OF BIRTH:** Lewisham, South London
4. **FAMILY:** Oldest of 5 children
5. **EDUCATION:** Alleyn's School, Dulwich, King's College, University of London
6. **TEENAGE AMBITION:** To get married and have a family
7. **CURRENT OCCUPATION:** Youth Officer for Dunkeld diocese
8. **TURNING POINT:** Discovering that no sin is greater than God's love

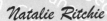

Natalie Ritchie

Natalie Ritchie's attacker disappeared into the darkness, leaving her lying in the middle of a muddy field far from her friends. The realisation that she had just been raped had not yet sunk in. She felt completely numb, devoid of emotion. It was the night of the school leavers' ball. Natalie should have been celebrating the end of her secondary education and looking to the future. Instead she was alone in the dark, the noise of the party blaring in the distance.

Scratched and bruised, she sat up in a daze. Her clothes were filthy, her hair a mess. Her first reaction was to blame herself for what had happened. She was drunk. Her defences were down, her normal inhibitions gone. Foolishly, she had allowed herself to be led away into a field where no one could see her. 'I told myself it was my fault', she recalls. She tried to put up a fight but soon realised it was pointless. 'I had a sense of resignation', she reveals. 'Mentally, I went somewhere else in my head. I didn't even feel upset. It was as if I didn't care.' Dragging herself up, Natalie staggered back to the ball. In the back of her mind was the fear that she might become pregnant. The next day she would need to take the morning-after pill to be sure she wouldn't conceive a baby. She would also need to have tests for sexually transmitted infections. In a state of profound shock, she rejoined her friends and drank herself into oblivion.

Natalie was born into a Catholic family in Lewisham, South London. Her parents were good Christians and the Ritchies attended Mass as a family most weeks. Outside Mass faith did not play much of a role in Natalie's life. She never went to confession. She didn't understand the sacraments of the Church and she never prayed with her family. Natalie's childhood was also blighted by sexual abuse. She claims she was repeatedly abused by a family member living nearby. Consequently, she found herself leading a double life. 'On the one hand, I had a nice, sheltered family life with lots of brothers and sisters. I used to look at my parents and think: "You don't really know me. I thought everyone else, even adults, had an innocence I didn't have. I felt dirty, like I had a dark secret to hide."'

She was 19 when she spoke to her parents for the first time about the abuse. The revelations, she says, almost led to the breakdown of their marriage. Through talking to other victims and a psychologist, Natalie believes that the abuse may have started very early in life, perhaps before she could even remember. She says it lasted for a period of five to six years.

At primary school she was bullied. She attended a Catholic state school in a tough catchment area. She was called names but also suffered physical abuse. She remembers being pushed down the stairs on one occasion. 'I was quite introverted', she explains. 'I found it hard to relate to my peers. I felt I was different but couldn't explain why. I told my parents about the bullying and they were very supportive. My reaction was to become a complete swot. I worked hard and won a full scholarship to a private school when I was eleven. My parents were really happy for me. The scholarship was my ticket out. No one was going there from my primary school.'

Natalie's dreams of making a fresh start were dashed when she took up her scholarship the following September. 'I was really different to everyone else again', she says. 'Because everyone else was wealthy and I was poor, I got bullied again'. Things went from bad to worse when Natalie visited a friend's house and was sexually abused by a second person. 'It confirmed all my worst fears', she says. 'It made me feel weird, dirty and unacceptable. Having since spoken to people in a similar situation, she knows that this is a pattern that occurs with many children who are abused. A child is more susceptible to abuse if they've been abused previously. I was eleven when I was sexually abused by another person. I didn't react. I just accepted it. I was preconditioned not to say anything. It happened on a few occasions over a period of two years. I didn't realise it wasn't the norm until I was about fourteen. Even then I rationalised what had happened by telling myself that other people had also suffered terrible things in life. I'd never been beaten up. I wasn't deprived socially. I didn't want to act like a victim. I didn't want a label attached to me. I felt it must have been my fault.'

In the classroom, Natalie was often in trouble with her teachers. She enjoyed studying but often got involved in blazing rows with teachers. 'I'd scream at them. No one could put their finger on why I behaved like this', she explains. 'I had a really strong sense of justice and injustice and I always felt like I was being bullied. If I felt like I was being picked on by teachers I'd go mental and make a massive fuss. It could be something as simple as being asked to stop talking. I'd always get moved to the front. I'd rebel by listening to my walkman in class and I once set fire to my bag. I was abnormal, sensitive to criticism and quite volatile.'

Natalie scored mostly As in both her GCSEs and A levels. Behind her wonderful academic record was an emotionally scarred teenager struggling to cope with the trauma of sexual abuse. This manifested itself in a desperate need to feel accepted by her peers. 'I'd had enough of feeling different to everyone', she recalls. 'I went to mad parties. I got really drunk. That became really important to me. It was a way of being normal because of the pain I suffered inside. It was therapeutic and it enabled me to have a social life and to blend in with other people. I always tried to get more wasted than anyone else. I started smoking weed, or cannabis, at the age of fourteen. I never touched cocaine or ecstasy. It wasn't that I was scared of hard drugs. I just didn't get beyond a bottle of vodka.' She adds: 'I developed a massive reliance on alcohol and cannabis. At one point I bunked off school every day. A friend lived opposite the school and we'd spend the day at her house getting wasted. My friend was going through a traumatic time. Her parents had swapped partners with another couple. It was chaos. Together, we were a recipe for disaster. Eventually, my friend made a horrible suicide attempt. She slit her wrists and I was the one who found her. I felt scared about leaving her alone after that. It caused a big downward spiral for me but I still had the sense of having had a religious or supernatural experience. I wondered if the Holy Spirit was at work. Although I had no knowledge or formation of my faith, I asked myself whether I'd been led to find her. It was very traumatic. I was relieved she was still alive.'

By the time she reached her fifteenth birthday, Natalie had several boyfriends on the go at once. At first she didn't have relationships, but soon realised she couldn't get close to members of the opposite sex without being sexually involved. Deep down she had an intense desire to be loved. 'I got really,

really used', she recalls, sadly. 'I didn't give away my sexuality easily. I didn't even have sex with the majority of them but things often went too far.'

Natalie had just turned fifteen when she first had sex with a boyfriend. 'I still had a strong conviction that sex before marriage was wrong', she says. 'My ideal was to get married, have a family and go to church. Waiting for the right person was something I valued so much.' But, high on alcohol and cannabis, Natalie had sexual intercourse with a man she had met in the pub. He was a Muslim war refugee from Bosnia. He was called Hassan and was two years her senior. Natalie had crossed a barrier in the heat of the moment and felt as if there was no turning back. She started going out with Hassan straightaway in an attempt to make sense of what had happened between them.

'We were together for three years', reveals Natalie. 'It was a really bad relationship. He was very frightening and controlling. I stayed with him out of fear and insecurity. We argued all the time and I was in tears every single day. At the time, I didn't see much of my friends or family. Many of my friends were getting into drugs, so he was my only stability. I never shared anything that happened in my childhood with him. He hit me on one occasion and shook me. I thought I was in love but we had nothing in common.' After a particularly bad argument, Natalie wanted to end the relationship. To confirm it was over she went off and slept with another young man who had been pursuing her for some time. Far from helping her to get over her relationship with Hassan, it plunged her into deeper turmoil. 'It happened on a council estate in Elephant and Castle, London. I felt totally numb. I had wanted to kick start my emotions because I was so messed up but I felt nothing. I didn't feel happy, sad or even shocked. It sounds melodramatic but I didn't actually care any more.'

In the depth of her despair, Natalie was desperately searching for answers. She decided one way out would be to make her confirmation. She joined a confirmation programme in her local parish. But the decision was made partly to distance herself from having had a relationship with a Muslim. In a confused state of mind, Natalie became involved with two men, one much older than herself, and slept with both of them. 'I felt like I couldn't go anywhere or do anything without causing a scandal', she recalls. 'I felt it was my fault'.

Natalie still made her confirmation but, despite admiring the faith of some of the people on her course, she wasn't touched on a deep spiritual level. 'I always believed that God and religion were important and eventually I would become a person who was into her faith. But it wasn't something I was actively pursuing. I was still very promiscuous.'

Things finally came to a head at the school leavers' ball in 2001. She was seventeen years old. Natalie was in a permanent state of numbness and the events that night plunged her into deeper despair. It was a beautiful evening and all her school friends were dressed up in ball gowns and suits. 'I couldn't be bothered', she says. 'I turned up in jeans and a t-shirt. There was a big marquee and I went round talking to people and getting drunk. I got talking to a particular guy. He led me away into a field and he started to pester me. I wasn't interested because I was having such an awful time with men at that time. I knew if we had sex that it wouldn't be safe. Neither of us had any condoms. He was very persistent but I repeatedly told him I didn't want to have sex. He was nagging and nagging and I was really drunk. He didn't hit me but he pushed me on to the ground and pulled off my clothes. He had sex with me and left me lying in the mud.'

Natalie's humiliation grew after the man who she claims assaulted her got up to leave. 'Incredible as it may seem, he gave me some advice. He said: "You need to wise up or that'll happen to you again and again. You're a pretty girl but you'll have to get a grip." I was worried about getting pregnant. He told me I was on my own. The following day, I took the morning-after pill - it wasn't the first time - and went for tests at a sexual health clinic.' Natalie says she was the victim of a 'date rape'. She explains: 'When people think of rape, they imagine a stranger jumping out of a shadowy place and sexually attacking them. Date rape is when forced sex happens between two people who know each other. It often happens in a college environment and alcohol and drug use is usually involved. I didn't even think of reporting what happened to the police. I had no witnesses and felt it would be my word against his.'

Although she didn't realise it at the time, Natalie had reached a crossroads in her life. God was about to lead her to him through another young person. This person would be Emilia Klepacka, a young Catholic student involved with Youth 2000. Natalie had known Emilia since the age of ten. The two had met through Focolare, a worldwide ecumenical movement. Natalie had come into contact with Focolare through an aunt.

'Emilia and I became really great friends', says Natalie. 'Because we lived so far away - Emilia in Hertfordshire and me in London - we didn't see each other very often. But we kept in touch and wrote to each other a lot over the years. Emilia was a real inspiration. I saw the way she lived her life and I hoped that one day I'd have the courage, faith and freedom to do the same. She had strong convictions that kept her on the straight and narrow, whereas I seemed to crumble into destructiveness. She was always meeting amazing people. She was someone who knew she was loved.'

One day, not long after the 'date rape' incident, Emilia phoned Natalie to say she was coming to London. She asked Natalie to meet her at Canning Town tube station. 'Emilia turned up in a car with two other people I didn't know. I got into the car with them. It was really weird because there was a rosary hanging on the mirror. We drove to a friary in east London. The door was opened by a friar wearing a long grey habit. I'd never seen a friar in my life. We went into the chapel there, where it was Holy Hour. I was really freaked out. I had never seen exposition of the Blessed Sacrament before. I didn't understand what was happening but it was really beautiful, very moving. What most struck me was seeing the friars, these big men, being humble and submissive before God.'

Afterwards, as Natalie sat down to dinner with Emilia and the others, one of the people she had met in the car described how he had turned to God after a life of extreme violence and crime. The man who spoke to her was John Pridmore, an ex-gangster in London's East End.

'It was like being in a weird dream', explains Natalie. 'John spoke about how sin clouds God's love. God doesn't go away but when there's a lot of sin in your life it's hard to see God. You only see the sin and the bad stuff. This was a complete revelation to me. John said sins were like wounds. I thought

God only loved good people. Before I'd always told myself: "When I become good and sort myself out, I can have this religion too". John spoke about confession too. As a child I'd made my first confession but was given general absolution. That evening I went to confession to Father Richard Roemer, one of the friars. It was the first time I'd ever confessed my sins to anyone. It was Easter 2001 and I felt like I'd walked out into a different world.'

Natalie couldn't face going home that night. She stayed with John Pridmore and his mum and went to Mass the following morning. As we went up to Holy Communion, John whispered: 'Remember, now you've been to confession you're as innocent as a newborn baby. I was very touched because I couldn't remember a time of innocence in my life.'

Natalie went home happy but struggled to understand many of the things that had happened to her in the short space of twenty-four hours. She was soon back in her normal routine and questioned whether her life had really changed. The following weekend she was invited to a Youth 2000 retreat in a nearby parish. She remembers sitting in the pub on the Friday night in two minds about whether to go. 'I was with a guy. It got to about 9 pm. I told myself: "I can still go to the retreat. I've got an option here." So I asked the guy to take me.'

As Natalie arrived, the Blessed Sacrament was carried in and everyone knelt down. 'There were so many young people and they were normal and reverent. They all had different stories.' Natalie started to grapple with the Catholic theology of transubstantiation - the doctrine that the whole substance of the bread and wine changes into the body and blood of Christ through a mystical process during consecration. 'I knew this intellectually but not in my heart. I'd never entertained the possibility that anyone actually believed in their heart that the Eucharist was the body and blood of Jesus Christ.'

That summer Natalie went to Youth 2000's annual prayer festival in Walsingham. In the months leading up to the retreat, she went to confession regularly and started to pray. Her biggest hurdle was not accepting that Jesus was present in the Blessed Sacrament but trying to leave behind her old way of life. 'Changing my lifestyle was the hardest part', she reveals. 'I still kept drinking and getting involved with men. I didn't know another life. None of my friends were Christians or had even been baptised.'

At Walsingham, Natalie felt deeply frustrated and observed how naturally prayer seemed to come to the other young people there. 'I felt dislocated and confused. I went to adoration but couldn't seem to put myself back together.' Then Father Stan Fortuna of the Franciscan Friars of the Renewal in

New York gave a talk and performed a rap song. 'The penny dropped', says Natalie. 'The pain I'd experienced wasn't separate from a religious conversion. God was with me in my pain and my life belonged to him. I still felt numb and hard inside but I started to cry. I was realising how powerful the God thing was. I saw myself as a whole person in front of God instead of being broken up into pieces. This was powerful enough to keep me going, knowing that God was big enough to contain me.'

Later Natalie spoke to Father Stan about her struggle to change her lifestyle and how she kept ending up in destructive relationships. 'He told me I was beautiful', she recalls. 'No one had said that to me before. By that, he meant that I was a child of God.' She also confided in him about the sexual abuse she had suffered in the past. She was deeply moved by his response. 'He told me I was precious and spoke about regaining the boundaries of self-respect. I struggled like any other young person to live this out but my lifestyle didn't go back to how it was before. I experienced a complete healing that enabled me to live the Christian life.'

A few weeks later Natalie started an English degree at King's College in London. At Walsingham she had met young people who were also students at the university. She went on retreat every weekend, quickly became involved with Youth 2000's music ministry and helped to lead retreats.

At the end of her first year, Natalie took a gap year to work for Youth 2000. John Pridmore invited her to join the mission team in Ireland, where she lived in community with six other young people from Ireland, Scotland and England. The community made promises of poverty, chastity and obedience.

'We lived off donations, slept on presbytery floors and didn't have any exclusive relationships', explains Natalie. 'It meant we couldn't have boyfriends and girlfriends while we were living in community.' Natalie and the others travelled all over Ireland, leading one-day retreats in schools and residential weekend retreats. The mission team followed a strict regime of prayer, Mass, adoration, the rosary, the Divine Office, and every evening they had an open examination of conscience when they would ask each other's forgiveness.

'It was really, really hard', reveals Natalie. 'But the pace at which we grew was amazing. I was nineteen at the time and close to the age of the young people we were working with. I discovered many people who'd had similar experiences to me. It was powerful to hear young people speak about the difficulties they had faced.'

Natalie gave her own powerful testimony of conversion to young people in schools and parishes in Ireland. At first they would often be shocked to see a young person of a similar age leading them in prayer. During the year, Natalie became close to Ruairi Dowey, a young Scot living in her community. 'He had also had a powerful conversion experience. Our friendship was leading to an exclusive relationship. We had to decide to stay in community with greater separation or to leave and pursue a romantic relationship', she says.

Natalie and Ruairi decided to leave the mission team. They got engaged in the summer of 2003. Natalie returned to London and combined her university studies with part-time youth work in parishes. She also began a course in parish catechesis at the Maryvale Institute in Birmingham. Since her conversion she has felt a strong call to work with young people.

She explains: 'It's about making yourself vulnerable and approaching young people as a human being. Young people are respectful and appreciate the fact that I'm speaking from the heart about my life. Faith then becomes something real and possible. I talk about relationships, chastity and marriage. Some young people will say to me: "That's wonderful but is it really possible?" That's exactly what I used to think. There's so much pain and destructiveness in youth culture, it's heartbreaking. There's an urgent need for leadership training and a strong voice to witness to the Church in today's society.'

At the time of writing this book, Natalie had just finished her English degree and was about to start a new job as a youth officer for Dunkeld diocese in Scotland. She and Ruairi, who is now training to be a psychiatric nurse, are planning to marry in December 2005.

Having met God in a personal way through adoration of the Blessed Sacrament, Natalie has been able to experience healing and forgive those she says abused her as a child and a teenager. 'The way I see it now is that these people have been damaged. To be in the position of an abuser, you must be living in total darkness. I pity someone trapped in that kind of horror. I've never had an apology or an acknowledgement of what I've suffered. I pray for them and I hope that one day, they'll experience healing too.'

Chapter 3

Rod Isaacs

CHANGED LIFE

Rod Isaacs

1. **NAME:** Rod Isaacs
2. **DATE OF BIRTH:** March 25th 1968
3. **PLACE OF BIRTH:** Godalming, Surrey
4. **FAMILY:** 1 of 5 children
5. **EDUCATION:** Charterhouse School, Goldaming, Cambridge University
6. **TEENAGE AMBITION:** To make a difference
7. **CURRENT OCCUPATION:** Student
8. **TURNING POINT:** A personal encounter with God

I t was new year 1990 and Rod Isaacs was feeling really fed up. Instead of having fun and getting drunk at a party, he was stuck on a pilgrimage with a group of people he hardly knew. He was in Medjugorje, in the former Yugoslavia, where six young visionaries claimed to have seen the Virgin Mary. Rod had just come out of the parish church and was feeling particularly disgruntled. He had strongly disagreed with a talk on priesthood and was arguing with a girl in the pilgrimage group. She suggested that they pray the rosary, but he snapped back: 'I'm not praying any more of that stupid prayer'.

In the middle of the afternoon when the sun was high in the sky, Rod went to the graveyard behind the church. A group of people had gathered there and were all staring at the sun. One girl was crying. Another was on her knees. Then someone shouted: 'Look, it's Jesus'. Rod glanced up into the sky and saw nothing except the sun. Yet those around him were still behaving strangely. Rod prayed: 'God, I don't know what's going on but if this is a sign from you, I want to see it'. His eyes were drawn to the sun, and after a while he realized he was looking at it without being blinded.

'Then I began to see all the colours of the rainbow around the perimeter of the sun', he reveals. 'All I could say was "Wow". The sun was a pure white disc clearly highlighted against a dark background. Then the disc began to rotate and spin faster and faster. There was a light spinning from it in all directions like a wheel of fire. The sun began to pulsate like a heart. And I was seeing all this with my own eyes. I felt an incredible sense of inner joy. God was totally there, radiating love. It was as if God was saying: "No part of the earth is too small to be showered with my grace. There's nothing more powerful than this love."' The vision of the sun reminded Rod of the host inside the monstrance during adoration of the Blessed Sacrament. Almost immediately, he started having doubts about what he had seen. Maybe he had got caught up in the hysteria? Could it have been an illusion? The only thing that convinced him it could be a genuine experience was the overwhelming joy he felt inside. He knew God was leaving him free to accept or reject this gift. Which path would he take?

Rod was born at home in Godalming, Surrey, and grew up in a close-knit family of five children. His dad was a non-practising Jew. His mum was Scottish, from a Presbyterian background, but later became an Anglican. Apart from celebrating the Jewish feast of the Passover each year, religion did not play a big role in Rod's childhood. His dad was strong on family traditions, and the table was seen as the most important place in the home. Both of his parents had a strong sense of natural justice and integrity. Rod's dad was a solicitor and sat on a solicitors' disciplinary tribunal. His mum was a magistrate.

Rod went to boarding school at the age of twelve. As a teenager, he was an introvert who questioned many things about the world. His surname made him a target for bullying and anti-semitism. At first Rod denied his Jewish background. He felt ashamed for allowing himself to be intimidated and slowly found the courage to stand up to the bullies. He became proud of his heritage and discovered other pupils who were also from a Jewish background.

Rod loved music and sang in the choir. He would also ponder the Christian meaning of some of the hymns. 'I didn't know whether it had any relevance to me', he says. 'I would ask myself whether people just liked the ceremony and the ritual of Christian services and what it meant in reality'. English was his favourite subject, and he was an avid reader. He was drawn to spiritual books and enjoyed reading about figures such as Mother Teresa and Martin Luther King. He would sometimes go to church to keep his mum company, but it did not touch him on a personal level. 'The Anglican church seemed like a hollow shell', he explains. 'I wouldn't say that now but that was the impression I got at the time'.

When he was thirteen some of his classmates were preparing for their confirmation. Rod asked his mum if he could be confirmed too. He had not been baptized as a child so he went to see a vicar. The meeting went badly. Rod wanted to hear about God, but the vicar insisted on talking to him about how his house was haunted by ghosts. Rod also went to talk to his school chaplain. He felt confused after he noticed the chaplain had an enormous Buddha statue in his hallway. The chaplain's reasons for being a Christian did not satisfy him.

Rod decided that baptism was not for him and poured his energy into his schoolwork. He took his A levels a year early and got a place at Cambridge to read English. Before starting university, he took a gap year and went travelling, first to India and then to Israel, where he lived in a *kibbutz*. 'I lived with a psychopathic Dutch guy who had been rejected from the army and got violent when he was drunk', he recalls. 'There were also a couple of guys from the East End who would smash a bottle during an argument'. He worked in a plastics factory and on a chicken farm. 'I'd have to get up at 3 a.m. to get the chickens ready for market. The smell was unbelievable.' After three months in the *kibbutz*, Rod visited all the important Christian sites of Israel and then went on to Egypt.

When he started at Cambridge the following autumn, he considered himself 'Mr Streetwise' and looked down on students who had not taken a gap year. One of his closest friends was Simon Bishop, an old boy from Stonyhurst College near Clitheroe in Lancashire. Simon, now a Jesuit priest, was the first Catholic Rod had ever met. He explains: 'I really didn't know what a Catholic was. I thought Catholics belonged to a sect and Anglicanism was Christianity.' Rod would grill Simon about Catholic issues. What was Mass? Why couldn't priests get married? 'Simon was very prayerful and involved with the Catholic chaplaincy', he says. 'At first I thought he was a bit too nice. I was waiting to see if he was genuine. Sometimes I went along to Mass with him. I loved the sense of mystery and watching people pray after communion but I wouldn't admit it to him. I situated myself as an outsider who came to observe.'

In the third year, Rod moved out of college and he and Simon shared a house together. 'Si was not like most students', he explains. 'If he met a homeless person on the street, he'd stop and talk to them. I'd try to do the same thing but I'd get really nervous. One day, I came home and there was an awful smell in the hallway. I shouted: "Hey Si, what have you been up to? Have you been eating too many baked beans?" He told me to keep my voice down because there was a homeless guy sleeping in his bed who had been roughed up during the night.'

During his final year, Simon and another friend, Robert Toone (Chapter 10), told Rod about Medjugorje. The supernatural events said to be happening there were the talk of the Catholic chaplaincy. Rod went along to discussions and video presentations which left him feeling both challenged and intrigued. He even handed out leaflets outside the English faculty, amused that he, an 'unbaptized pagan', was encouraging people to attend Christian talks. In a strange twist of fate, one of the videos featured his future wife, Ann Marie, a young Irishwoman who had been touched by Medjugorje. 'I knew Robert was keen on her but I remember saying: "If I ever marry anyone, I hope she's like "that Irish girl". I didn't think for a minute that I'd ever meet her, let alone marry her.'

As Rod approached his finals, he experienced a period of existential anguish. He felt something was missing in his life. He realized it was God. He left Cambridge in 1989 desperate to share some of 'this faith' he had witnessed in young students over the last three years. He was filled with anxiety and didn't know what to do as a career. In the end, he took up a place to study journalism at Cardiff and began a year of intensive training. By now his search for God was at the forefront of his life. He went to Mass every Sunday, prayed the rosary and read widely about Medjugorje. In his journalism he was constantly searching for spiritual subjects.

Towards the end of 1989, Rod decided to go to Medjugorje. He spoke to Robert, who put him in touch with Amanda Godwin, who was organising a pilgrimage in the New Year. At first Rod found the pilgrimage tough and challenging. 'I gave Amanda a hell of a time', he reveals. 'I was constantly arguing with her. There was a lot of fear inside me. I knew God was real but I didn't know him on a personal level.' Rod was at a low ebb when he reluctantly decided to go and pray in the graveyard. The last thing he expected was to see the sun dance in the sky. It was the sign he needed to take him forward in his faith journey. Medjugorje was the turning point. 'There was an extraordinary sense of God's presence', he says. 'It was like heaven had come to earth'.

For months after he had been to Medjugorje, Rod would feel an enormous sense of joy welling up inside when he reflected on his experiences there. After finishing his journalism course, he moved to London to work for a third world economics magazine. He attended a prayer group and became involved with Youth 2000. 'My first ever retreat was exhilarating and inspiring', he recalls. 'It was very charismatic with lots of praise and worship. I thought Youth 2000 was the Catholic Church and this was normal. I was educated in prayer by Youth 2000 and it gave me confidence to play the guitar at a prayer group in Kensington. I would have been at sea without

Youth 2000. I made so many friends. Youth 2000 was my spiritual family.'

It was around this time that Rod decided to become a Catholic. 'I wanted my dad's blessing but I was terrified about asking him for it', he recalls. 'When I asked him, he was wounded but very gracious. Somewhere in his psyche I was betraying my Jewish heritage. I was going to the other side.' For Rod, Christianity felt like the fulfilment of his spiritual journey. Today his wedding ring bears a Hebrew inscription.

Rod was baptized and received into the Catholic Church in 1992. His old Cambridge friend Simon Bishop, who had played such a big part in the lead up to his conversion, was his sponsor. The previous autumn, Rod had given up journalism to become a teacher. His first job was teaching English at the London Oratory, where he stayed for four years. Rod also helped with the homeless and started a prayer group at St Mary of the Angels Church in Bayswater. The parish priest there was Father Michael Hollings, who was also known for giving up his bed for homeless and destitute people.

'I got stuck into all things Catholic', says Rod. 'It was an intense period of my life. I was struggling to come back down to earth. I was still on a high after my conversion experience.'

He began to wonder if he might have a vocation to the priesthood. He made a few enquiries and visited the Franciscan Order in Chilworth, Surrey. The visit did not go well and Rod felt very confused. 'I started going out with a girl but felt like I was running away from my fear of commitment', he says. 'I knew she wasn't the one for me but worried I wouldn't find anyone else'.

Rod was introduced to Ann Marie Lyons, the young woman he had admired on the Medjugorje video some years previously. They attended an international Taizé gathering together in Paris at the end of 1994. 'I fell in love with Ann Marie instantaneously', he reveals. 'I experienced such joy being with her and talking to her. I put Ann Marie through hell with the priesthood business. We both suffered because we loved each other and didn't know where it was leading.'

After the Taizé meeting, Rod decided to stop seeing Ann Marie and spend some time discerning his vocation in life. He gave up teaching and sought advice from Father Hollings, who suggested he spend some time at a remote hermitage near Edinburgh. Rod ended up spending a month with two elderly hermits, Father Roland, a Catholic priest, and Father John, an Anglican vicar. He led an intense prayer life which involved rising each morning at 4 a.m. to pray in a hut chapel. 'I discovered the degree to which I didn't love myself', he explains. 'I realized I was afraid of God and didn't love or trust him enough'.

Towards the end of his stay, Rod was paralysed with fear. 'I was so afraid of making the wrong decision that I couldn't decide what to do with my life. I really wanted to get to know Jesus better. I knew I had to find him in the poor. I felt a strong desire to serve the poor.' Rod made a list of twelve organizations which could help him live out this vocation. They included an interfaith *kibbutz* in Israel, a Catholic charity, an inner-city Anglican parish and *L'Arche*, an international federation of communities for people with learning disabilities.

Rod realized he had now reached a crossroads in his life. He turned to Father Roland for help. He decided to put the twelve organizations into a hat and pick one out. He went away and prayed: 'God, please make sure I pick the right thing'. Father Roland heard Rod's confession and then they prayed the Our Father. Rod put the scraps of paper with the names of the organizations on top of the Bible on the altar. 'Roland said: "Are you ready yet?" I said: "No, let's say another Our Father". Then I reached out, picked one of the bits of paper and it said *L'Arche*.'

Immediately Rod felt that he had chosen the right path. The previous year he had visited *L'Arche* in Trosly, near Compiègne in France. 'I went into this beautiful open plan house', he recalls. 'There was no one around. I walked into the living-room and there was a guy with Down's syndrome, rocking backwards and forwards with his tongue out and chuckling to himself. I tried to be warm and friendly to him but felt really nervous. I said "Bonjour", and he laughed. I felt so handicapped. He looked at me again, and I noticed he was very short. He stood up, led me to an armchair and sat me down. He crouched down and put his arms on my knees. That was the position we were in when the assistants came in for supper. His name was Christophe. I knew it had been an important moment for me but I was desperately afraid of it.'

Rod joined the Trosly community on 19 March 1996, the feast of St Joseph. He had chosen Joseph as his confirmation name and felt the saint was now guiding him. 'I discovered God in the everyday washing, cooking, cleaning and changing of nappies', he says. He took part in a BBC Everyman documentary on the community and received spiritual direction from *L'Arche's* founder, Jean Vanier.

Then one day, out of the blue, he received a letter from Ann Marie telling him that her brother would be getting married in Ireland during the summer of 1997. 'Part of me had shut Ann

Marie out of my life. I didn't know how to deal with her letter so I didn't reply.' Rod was due to go to Ireland for a stag party around the time of her brother's wedding. He decided he would wait until he got to Ireland to contact Ann Marie. 'It was lovely to hear her voice', he says. 'She said she had passed her driving test and would drive down from her parents' home in Co. Roscommon to Galway to see me. I was in a complete state because I had been thinking *L'Arche* was my vocation. I met Ann Marie and knew she was still really important to me. I said to her: "I know we'll always be friends". I was gutless and couldn't take the plunge.'

Rod didn't see Ann Marie again until World Youth Day in Paris later that year. 'I bumped into her in a church where Youth 2000 was present. We talked and Ann Marie told me she had just been to confession. At the end the priest had asked her if she wanted to marry me. When she finally said "Yes", he said: "Well, tell him". So that's what she did. She really laid it on the line, but she also said: "I can't see you anymore unless we're going to get married". So I was left mumbling: "I do love you and if I marry anyone it'll be you, but I'm just not sure I'm called to be married. I knew I'd better make up my mind so I told Ann Marie I'd go to Medjugorje and pray. I said I'd call her as soon as I got some clarity. I wanted to have God's affirmation. I prayed and fasted for two weeks in Medjugorje. It felt like a huge weight had been lifted from my shoulders. I felt as if God was saying: "This is what I'm offering you. I'm asking you if you want to be with Ann Marie for the rest of your life." I phoned Ann Marie and said: 'Let's get married.'

Rod proposed to Ann Marie in November 1997 in the chapel of *L'Arche* community in Trosly. They married the following September in Ireland. Their first daughter Miriam Rose was born on 25 June 2000, the anniversary of the Medjugorje apparitions. Their second daughter, Elsa Thérèse, was born on 21 June 2003, the feast of St Aloysius Gonzaga, a patron saint of youth.

For five years Rod worked as a parish youth co-ordinator at St Joseph's Church, Gerard's Cross, near London. In September 2004, Rod, Ann Marie and their family set out on a new adventure abroad. They are now living in Gaming, a mountain village near Vienna where Rod is studying for a master's degree in theological studies on marriage and the family. At the end of the course, Rod hopes to use his degree to work in a related field for the Church in England and Wales. Until then he will keep stepping out in faith.

Chapter 4
Josie Callaghan

'Quick, call an ambulance,' shouted one voice. 'Is she alive?' screamed another. A crowd had gathered around the mangled wreckage of an old green Mini. Stuck inside was a young woman who was drifting in and out of consciousness. Minutes earlier the car had spun off the road at 60 m.p.h. straight into a tree. As the emergency services arrived at the scene, Josie Callaghan was rapidly losing consciousness. It took an hour before firefighters could cut her free from the wreckage. Even then, the roof of the car had to be completely removed before she could be rescued.

It was 6 June 1995 and Josie was travelling back to university in Southampton. She remembers little about the day's events apart from pulling over to read a road map. When she came round in hospital, Josie discovered she had been lucky not to have died in the accident or to have broken her spine. For the first nine weeks, she was in traction. She spent the next three weeks in a wheelchair. Her injuries were horrific. 'I had broken virtually every limb in my body', she recalls. 'I broke ribs, my eye orbit, fingers and nose. I broke my left knee badly. I also broke my femur, right ankle and left lower arm.' She has since had 30 operations to reconstruct her skeleton, mostly in the lower body, and she still suffers from double vision in her right eye when looking to the far right.

While Josie was in hospital, she was visited by a driver who had witnessed the accident. 'He told me that my car had touched the kerb. I had tried to right it but swerved into the oncoming traffic', she says. 'I tried to right it again but veered too far to the left and hurtled into a field and hit the only tree in it.' She was also told that a woman who happened to work for the ambulance service had been passing at the time of the accident. The woman had been first on the scene and had dialled 999.

To this day, Josie isn't certain what caused the crash. She presumes that the brakes on her mini failed. A few weeks before the accident her sister's boyfriend had fitted *Sirocco* racing seats inside the front of the car. They are designed to protect the driver in case of an impact but Josie didn't think she needed them. With hindsight, she is convinced the seats saved her life. She also believes that God had plans for her and had spared her life for a reason.

Josie was brought up by her mum. Her dad, who is Irish, travelled extensively with his job and her parents eventually separated. When she was nine months old, Josie's mum returned to her native Nigeria taking with her Josie and her older sisters, Lynette and Celia. 'I don't remember much about that time except that I was happy and we were living with my grandmother', says Josie. The three pillars of the Callaghan household were education, faith and family. 'I had a very happy childhood from a spiritual point of view', recalls Josie. 'I always felt a closeness to Our Lord and Mary. My mum's example instilled that in me.'

When she was eight, Josie's family returned to England. At home she would help out with her younger siblings, Winston, Laura and Matilda. The family had now grown to six children, and every summer the Callaghans would go back to Nigeria on holiday.

In 1989, 19 year-old Josie's life was struck by tragedy when her eldest sister Lynette died in a motorbike accident during a holiday in Greece. Josie was helped through the ordeal by her mum's great strength of character and faith. 'I saw my mum living her faith through good times and bad. That helped me to cope,' she says.

It wasn't until she went to university that Josie's own faith was seriously challenged. As she was desperate to mix in and be part of the crowd, religion started to take a back seat. 'I was a one-hour Catholic', she laughs. 'By that I mean I went to Mass once a week at university and didn't give much thought to my faith for the rest of the week. I had a good set of friends and would go clubbing and drinking. I did enjoy myself.'

Underlying all her student experiences was the desire to be liked by her peers. 'I loved to be the life and soul of the party. I wanted to be the centre of attention. I was the one who tried to make people laugh and would make the crudest jokes.' Fit and active, Josie played squash and attended aerobics classes. Her physical appearance was important to her. Like most young people her age she was hoping for a close relationship with someone of the opposite sex.

After Josie graduated with a degree in biochemistry and organic chemistry from London University, she began a Ph.D. in biochemistry at Southampton. The gap between her student lifestyle and faith continued to widen. 'It became a real issue', she says. 'I went to Mass but people would joke about my faith'. As a postgraduate Josie had boyfriends but she never felt fulfilled in her relationships. 'There was always a tension', she recalls. 'That perhaps came from not being with someone who shared my beliefs. I felt as if I was wearing a mask.'

She had known her first boyfriend for nearly three years before she started dating him. When the relationship broke down after four months, Josie felt crushed. 'He was a Catholic and he would make fun of the faith. Although I wasn't in love with him, I found it hard to cope with rejection and for a while

I felt very hurt.' Her next relationship developed after she became the sympathetic ear for a young man who had just broken up with his girlfriend. 'Again, the relationship didn't last for long because I wasn't at peace. I wasn't happy in either of these relationships. They weren't mature.'

By June 1995, Josie had finished her practical work for her Ph.D. and just had to complete her thesis. She had been to a conference in Boston and applied for a job with Carlsberg in Copenhagen. The previous month, she had treated herself to a new car. She had bought an old Mini for cash and was looking forward to using it to drive to London for the baptism of her niece, Soraya. Shortly after buying the car, she had noticed the brakes were 'soft' but never got round to getting them checked. She had not been keen when her sister's boyfriend had insisted on fitting the Sirocco seats to the car. She found them uncomfortable. When she returned to Southampton she would take the car to a garage, have the brakes checked and get the seats removed. But it wasn't meant to be.

Josie was travelling along the A272 Winchester road from London when her car crashed into a tree. Remarkably, she didn't feel anxious or worried before losing consciousness. The accident marked a turning-point in her life. 'I felt that God took me out of my previous life and gave me a new one', she reveals. 'I thank God for that today. I feel fulfilled and excited about the future.'

In hospital, Josie never had time to wallow in self-pity. 'There were so many things to cope with that I just had to get on with them'. Back at home, life was not so easy. 'When I got back to my mum's, I looked in the mirror and saw that my eye was sunken. I had a bow leg and one thigh was round like a ball.' Josie became distressed by her physical appearance. Physiotherapy helped to restore her confidence but it was her mum who was once again the 'heroine of the story'. 'She didn't allow me to wallow. She pointed out that I wasn't paralysed and that I could walk. She told me: "Snap out of it, God's here". I always knew that everything she said came with sympathy. It wasn't a house for self-pity. It did help me to get on with things.'

For a while, there were still ups and downs and Josie had to struggle against her will. 'I did still wallow and there were times when I wanted to lie in bed and escape the world. I realized I would be stuck forever with the body I now have. I was very preoccupied by my physical limitations and how I looked.'

Josie finished her thesis from home and was awarded a Ph.D. For all her academic success, she was still unsure what to do with her life. 'I feel intelligence comes out of how you grow through life experiences, using it to relate to others rather than it being about how many qualifications you have', she says.

'To stay on the right track humility is imperative in the world of academia and it's very hard to do. After all that why do I have a Ph.D.? Because I didn't know what to do with my life, I enjoyed the life of being a student and it pleased my family.' The accident also helped Josie gradually to see her life in a new light. 'I didn't wake up one day with the idea that I'd almost died', she says. 'I felt that it wasn't my time. Over the course of time, I realized my faith had deepened.'

The first step in Josie's deepening of faith was a retreat at the House of Prayer in Co. Tyrone, Ireland. After an initial visit with her family, Josie and her younger sister, Laura, went for a second time and stayed a whole month. 'It was the real beginning of my life as it is now. I wanted to know God. I wanted him to take control.'

On their return to London, Josie and Laura decided to rent a house together in Plaistow. Josie became concerned when Laura started to attend a Youth 2000 prayer group. 'Laura was vanishing two or three times a week', laughs Josie. 'The first time I went along was to rescue her from some sort of cult she'd become involved with.'

Josie soon changed her mind about Youth 2000 after she attended her first retreat in Ilford, Essex, in 1997. 'I was blown away. I had never before contemplated the Lord through Eucharistic adoration.' Josie had been to Benediction as a child but had not fully understood that Jesus was present in the Blessed Sacrament. At the Youth 2000 retreat, adoration took on a whole new meaning. She was also touched by the testimony of John Pridmore, a former gangster in London's East End (Chapter 5).

Josie began to wonder if she might have a religious vocation. In 1998 she made two visits to the Community of the Beatitudes in Mortain, France. 'There was a realization that I was being called to a community. Before that time, I knew I would never get married but I still desired marriage. When I was in France, I started to desire community life.'

At the same time, Josie was worried about how she would cope with the structure of community life. The head of the community encouraged her to go away and pray, find a spiritual director and learn French before making a decision.

Back in London, she told John Pridmore about how she felt called to community. 'He said there was something about to start up in Leeds. I didn't know whether to take him seriously.' John turned out to be right. Youth 2000 was about to set up a community near Leeds which would work as a mission team, evangelizing in schools and parishes and organizing retreats across the country.

Josie and a friend from London, Mary Aldridge, decided to join the Youth 2000 community for a year. Josie and Mary had attended a prayer group in Tottenham Hale, which was attached to the House of Prayer in Ireland. They had also become interested in Youth 2000 at about the same time.

Josie hoped that the year in community in Leeds would help to confirm her calling to the Beatitudes. 'Once in Leeds, I felt as if I became my true self', she says. Josie and Mary joined Gina Hutchings, a doctor, and Clare Ward, a former BBC journalist, on the team (Chapter 6). They ran the Youth 2000 office from a spare room at the home of Robert Toone, director of Youth 2000, and his wife, Amanda (Chapter 10). Over the next year they organized 22 retreats, one in each diocese.

An anonymous donation meant that the mission team had enough money to rent a house for the year in the Yorkshire village of East Keswick where Robert and Amanda were based. 'I'd said I wouldn't join the community unless I had my own room', says Josie. 'At the time I was still awaiting reconstructive surgery following the accident. It was all divine providence. That year really did teach me how God works.'

The community was constantly praying for donations to finance the running of retreats. 'We were always praying for healthy amounts', recalls Josie. 'For example, we would need £15,000 in two weeks. We would pack up the office and go and pray in the chapel until the donations arrived. For me the words of the gospel came alive.'

The nature of the work meant that the mission team spent long periods of time on the road, travelling around the country in a van. 'We would literally finish a retreat in Truro, Cornwall, jump in the van and arrive in Birmingham at 2 a.m. ready to run a retreat for 1200 schoolchildren the following day.'

Josie felt so happy and at peace living in community that she decided to stay on for an extra year. Gina decided to give up her job as a doctor and joined the Community of St John, near St Etienne in France. Clare joined the Community of the Beatitudes and Mary returned to London.

Josie was asked to run the new mission team. Members included John Pridmore, Paul Bray, now a seminarian at Ushaw, Declan Jones, a tree surgeon, Catherine Underwood, now a contemplative nun in an enclosed order (Chapter 8), Catherine Vooght, a nurse, Emilia Klepacka, who was on a gap year before taking up a place at Cambridge University and Erin Flaherty from the United States. Frances Pollard joined in the summer of 2001 and later found a vocation with the Sisters of the Renewal, the female counterpart to the Franciscan Friars of the Renewal in New York.

'We had huge, tense moments and ups and downs but there was a real enthusiasm and a real love of God', says Josie. 'That's what kept us together. We spent an hour in adoration each day, even when we were on the road and had been up from 6 a.m. It was hard and the lifestyle challenged us. There were no exclusive relationships, which was tough. The fact was that we were committing ourselves to spreading the gospel.'

On a Friday night at the beginning of a weekend retreat, Josie would often be overcome with anxiety. 'I would say: "Lord, I've taken on too much". On the Sunday, I would be moved to tears when I listened to the testimonies of these young people.' There were many stories of young people who had experienced conversion. Some had been involved in the occult or self-mutilation. Others had suffered from depression and previously attempted suicide. There were those who had been hurt through abusive relationships or family breakdown. There were also alcoholics and drug addicts.

At the beginning of 2003, Josie helped Youth 2000 to launch a school of evangelization. Eleven young people signed up for the first intensive five-week course of study, prayer and community living. 'It was about helping young people to discover that what the Catholic faith professes is both reasonable and above reason. These days young people want to understand with their heads as well as their hearts.' One student left to pursue a vocation and the remaining ten stayed on to work as full-time volunteers on the mission team in the run-up to the annual summer prayer festival in Walsingham.

Josie's own experience at the heart of Youth 2000 helped her to realize that she wasn't being called to the Beatitudes in France but to a community life much closer to home.

In September 2003, she left Leeds to spend a year in London and contemplate her future. She joined Cornerstone, a lay community in Whitechapel that helps young women discern their vocation in life. Josie also began a full-time job as relationship manager for Alpha for Catholics in the UK. Alpha runs a series of courses which address the key issues of the Christian faith. She was one of two Catholics on the 150-strong Alpha team.

At the time of writing this book, Josie was planning to return to Youth 2000 and begin a new lay community. 'I would love to consecrate myself under private vows', she explains. 'I feel called to give myself to Jesus in a public way. The intimacy I crave is with Jesus. Community is so important. I feel that, if it's God's will, a long-term community will be set up that young people can feed into. It needs to be a signpost and a support. Youth 2000 gives young people that first trigger, that flame of desire to be with Christ. It's a gateway or a stepping stone in their journey of faith. Community helps people to find their true selves but it doesn't end there. It's only the beginning.'

Chapter 5

John Pridmore

CHANGED LIFE

1. **NAME:** John Pridmore
2. **DATE OF BIRTH:** February 4th 1964
3. **PLACE OF BIRTH:** Hackney, London
4. **FAMILY:** 1 of 2 sons, parents divorced
5. **EDUCATION:** Chapel End Secondary School, Walthamstow, Reading Court, Harold Hill
6. **TEENAGE AMBITION:** To be a champion pool player
7. **CURRENT OCCUPATION:** Youth 2000 evangelist in Ireland
8. **TURNING POINT:** Hearing the voice of God in his heart after nearly killing a man

John Pridmore

Slamming the door shut behind him, John Pridmore had arrived home with a pack of lagers tucked under his arm, ready for a quiet night in. He flung down his keys on the kitchen table, turned on the lights in his luxury flat and opened a can of beer. He took a few swigs on the way to the lounge and then sank down into the comfy leather armchair. He lit a cigarette, picked up the remote control, turned on the TV and flicked through the channels. It had been two weeks since he had been charged with grievous bodily harm after beating a man senseless on a pavement outside a pub. Taking a drag from his cigarette, he felt really low and thought how hopeless his life had become. He was a gangster who was feared throughout London's East End. He had the best sports cars, a string of good-looking girls and everything else money could buy. But he felt dead inside.

Then suddenly he heard a voice speaking in his heart. Terrified, he looked around the flat but no one was there. He checked to see if the TV was still on, switched channels and turned it off. The voice was still there, listing all the terrible things he had done in his life. John realized God was talking to him. It was as if he had journeyed into the mouth of hell and God's love had been totally withdrawn from him. It was the darkest moment of his life. 'I realized God was real', he recalls. 'I cried out for another chance not because I was sorry but because I didn't want to stay in that desolation. From that moment God came alive. I had the greatest buzz ever. It was the Holy Spirit, better than any drugs I had ever taken.'

John had a strong urge to go and stand outside his flat. He felt enveloped by peace and love and uttered his first prayer. 'God, up until now all I've ever done is take from you', he said. 'Now I want to give'. It was past one a.m, but John was desperate to share his experience with someone. The only people he knew who believed in God were his mum and his stepdad. Half an hour later he was at their house, knocking on the door. 'Mum, I think I've found God', he said, as she opened the door, bleary-eyed.

John grew up in Walthamstow in East London. His dad was a policeman and had been brought up in the Church of England. His mum, a shop assistant, was a practising Catholic. Although she later drifted away from her faith, John and his elder brother, David, were baptized into the Catholic Church. John had a happy childhood until the age of ten, when his parents divorced. 'They said I could choose who I wanted to live with,' says John. 'I decided then that I wouldn't love any more because then I wouldn't get hurt'.

In the weeks that followed John's mum had a nervous breakdown and was admitted to a psychiatric hospital. John lived with his dad and would visit his mum first at the hospital and later at a rehabilitation hostel. After John developed a rash, thought to be caused by stress, the doctor suggested that he stop visiting his mum until the rash subsided. John didn't see her for a period of six months. In the meantime, his dad had struck up a friendship with Elsie, the mother of one of his schoolfriends. His dad and Elsie moved in together. There were now five children under one roof. It wasn't long before rows started. 'My stepmum thought real discipline was important for children', says John. 'Although she wasn't physically violent, the bringing of the two families together was violent. I lost a lot of love from my dad. Instead of behaving well, I saw that being bad and getting into trouble got me attention.'

After John's mum was discharged from the hostel, he would often spend the weekend with her. She was now dating a man called Alan. It was during this time that John began shoplifting. Spurred on by the excitement, he became more adventurous, mostly stealing useless items just for fun. Things got worse after he and two friends started to break into schools, factories and shops. They were eventually caught after they broke into John's school to steal dinner money during the summer holidays. Finding all the doors to the classrooms and offices locked, they smashed everything in sight, causing thousands of pounds worth of damage.

Two days later two police officers arrived at John's house with a search warrant. They found a number of stolen items under John's bed. He was arrested and sentenced to three months in a detention centre. After his release, he turned again to crime, stealing money from the till at work and breaking into colleges – anywhere he could get his hands on large sums of cash.

John was due to leave school the following Easter and had no idea what to do with his life. The owner of an electrical shop, where he had worked as a Saturday boy since the age of fifteen, offered him a full-time job. His boss bought him his first motorbike and would allow John to pay him back £5 a week. John had an accident when he was sixteen after losing control of his motorbike. He broke his leg in 28 places and dislocated his snoulder and spent several months in hospital. He was visited by the hospital chaplain, but the priest never spoke to him about God. His mum and Alan had also started going back to Mass and his stepdad would talk to him about the love of God. 'Looking back at my life, I realize that could have been an opportunity', he says.

Instead, John became more angry with himself and those around him. One day, not long after he had returned to work, his boss sent him out to get a spare set of keys cut. John got an extra set done for himself. In the early hours of the morning when no one was about, he broke into the shop and stole hi-fis and blank video tapes. He would also steal money from the till when his employer was out for lunch.

A year later John was breaking into the shop as usual when he was caught by the police. 'I remember it being near to Christmas', he explains. 'I let myself in. I turned off the alarms. I was stealing dozens of items when the police came in, pointed a torch and arrested me. I was bundled into the van, aware that a lot of them would have known my dad.'

John was held overnight in custody and charged the following day. He pleaded guilty and was sent to a young offenders' institution. He was 19 years old. Once in his prison cell, pain flared up in the leg he had broken in the motorbike accident. 'My leg was ulcerated and I'd been in and out of hospital several times with it,' he says. 'I spent most of the time in solitary confinement. I was on my own fighting the pain. I seriously thought about topping myself.'

John was also racked with guilt about his former employer. 'My boss had been really kind to me. I'd spent three years working for him. I realized how much I'd hurt him. I really began to hate myself. I wrote a letter to my dad to say sorry for being such a disaster of a son. I wrote a similar letter to my mum. I was in Ipswich and my dad came all the way from London to see me.'

After he left prison, John tried to sell some filing cabinets he had picked up from a skip to an office furniture shop. The shop was owned by a 59-year-old man called 'Bulldog'. 'We clicked straightaway', says John. 'I was having a laugh with him. I didn't know he was one of the biggest faces in East London. I'm a big guy and he liked having big people around him. It gave him security. He said to me: "You're a big lad. Do you want to work for me?"'

Bulldog introduced him to his son, Ray, and John began work as a bouncer. 'I worked at clubs with him and we also did backstage security at concerts for bands like Queen and Simply Red. It was a ticket to supplying tons and tons of drugs. The cars outside would be filled with cocaine, sulphate, or speed, and ecstasy. We worked on a lot of doors where the drug dealers could get in easily. If they were spotted by security then we had to get them out. Our only concern was the drugs, worth thousands and thousands of pounds. If it had come to a choice between Freddie Mercury and one of our guys, Freddie wouldn't have stood a chance.' John and his associates also watched carefully to make sure other drug dealers weren't stealing their patch. 'If we saw someone who shouldn't have been there, we'd hurt them'.

John was sometimes sent to Dover to pick up drugs direct from the ferry. 'I'd take a black cab from London and then drive back in a Land Rover packed with drugs. I'd get paid about £1,000 for the job. Bulldog made me do these trips to test my loyalty.' John began to mix with hardened criminals who had stabbed and shot people. Violence, drug dealing, protection rackets and debt collecting were all part of his life. He worked as a go-between for three of London's most vicious underground 'firms'. He explains: 'All of the firms operated on tip-offs from corrupt policemen who would be paid for their information with new houses and cars'.

At the height of his gangster lifestyle, John wielded a machete and a knuckle duster. A can of ammonia was stuffed into one trouser pocket and wads of money were packed into the other. He wore designer suits, drove a Mercedes with a personalized number plate and lived in a penthouse flat. He was earning thousands of pounds a week and could sleep with virtually any woman he chose. He constantly picked fights and turned on anyone who got in his way. 'When you're living that sort of life, there's a lot of self-hatred', he says. 'Although I was violent outwardly, I was scared inside so I became more violent'.

It was summer 1991 when John finally hit rock bottom. He was working as a bouncer at a popular pub in the West End. He ended up arguing with a drinker at closing time before beating him up and leaving him lying in a pool of blood on the pavement outside. 'I thought I'd killed him', he recalls. 'When I got back to my flat I thought about what I'd become' .

John's life slowly started to unravel. Drink, drugs, glue sniffing and gambling were his 'painkillers'. He reveals: 'The painkillers had to become stronger. I moved on to crack and smoked an eighth of dope a day. I started questioning why nothing made sense any more.' John was awaiting trial for GBH on the night he heard God speaking in his heart. Feeling depressed, he had gone home earlier than usual. He had absolutely no inkling that this would be the night that would change his life.

As John sat round the kitchen table with his mum and stepdad in the early hours of the morning, he described what had happened to him back at the flat. His mum then made an extraordinary revelation. 'She told me she'd prayed for me every day but recently she had felt her prayers weren't being answered. She said: "I prayed to Jesus to take you. If it meant dying, then to let you die, but not to let you hurt yourself or anyone else any more."' His mum had even prayed to St Jude, the patron saint of hopeless cases. His stepdad, who died in 1998, gave John a copy of the Bible. 'The first page I turned to was the Prodigal Son', he recalls.

The following day, John went to see his mum's parish priest, Father Denis Hall. 'First of all, he reassured me this was a genuine conversion from God', says John. 'He really believed me. He suggested that I went to Aylesford Priory on retreat. He gave me £20. He didn't realize that I had thousands and thousands of quid. I didn't want to tell him what my life was really like.'

A few days later, John set off for a five-day retreat at the priory in Kent. 'I took a great big lump of dope with me', he reveals. 'I met a guy who'd been a heroin addict and he told me how he had completely changed his life. He told me to stop taking drugs.' John began to reassess his life and decided he would also give away all of his wealth.

Back in London, he distanced himself from Bulldog and the firms with whom he had been involved in organized crime. He took up voluntary work with the elderly at a drop-in centre. John went to church once every few weeks but struggled with the Catholic Church's teaching. He found Mass boring and couldn't understand why the Church wouldn't let divorced people remarry. He also questioned papal authority and the Vatican's wealth. 'I remember going into one church and picking up a magazine. Inside I saw a form about becoming a missionary priest. I filled it in and sent it off.'

Father Michael Kelly of the Kiltegan Fathers, a missionary order, came to visit John in his luxury flat. 'He would have seen all the guns and machetes on the wall', says John. 'The first thing he told me was I'd have to go to confession. I told him: "I'm not confessing to you". I thought he'd hate me. But Father Michael wasn't someone who was scared of telling the truth. He told me I needed to make my confirmation and seriously think about getting some education, sitting some O levels and A levels, if I wanted to be a priest. Then he invited me to go on a Youth 2000 retreat at Pentecost.'

John decided to take up the invitation. The day before he was due to set off for the retreat, nine policemen turned up at his front door and arrested him. 'I owed £2,700 in fines', he chuckles. 'I was taken to the Magistrates' Court. I said I could only pay £1 a week because I was doing voluntary work at the time. Not wanting to wait 2,700 weeks for the money, I was sent to Pentonville prison for 30 days.'

Throughout his imprisonment, John prayed the rosary and invited his cell mate to join in. John wrote to Father Michael to explain why he hadn't been able to attend the retreat. 'He must have had a good laugh at my excuse: "But Father, I was in prison",' he recalls, breaking into laughter. 'Father Michael wrote back to say there was another retreat, this time at

Aylesford. I thought this was amazing because I'd already been there.'

The Aylesford retreat marked another turning-point for John. Although he had been baptized a Catholic, he had not been to confession for 27 years. During the retreat he spent an hour confessing. Afterwards he attended Mass but felt confused about the Eucharist. 'I didn't understand that this piece of bread was meant to be Jesus', he says. 'I prayed: "Lord, if this is really you, help me to understand". Then, I had that same feeling I had outside the flat. I knew that it was Jesus really present.'

The following year, John went on his second Youth 2000 retreat and there he consecrated his heart to Mary, the mother of God. He worked on the Kingsmead Estate in Hackney, which was voted the worst estate in Europe two years running. After two and a half years there he joined the Craig Lodge community in Dalmally, Scotland, where he would pray for three hours a day. In 1998 he returned to London and did a short stint as a Youth 2000 regional leader before testing a vocation with the Franciscan Friars of the Renewal in the Bronx. After six months in the States, John felt God was calling him back to England to work with 'kids who were broken'.

For the next two years John worked as a full-time evangelist for Youth 2000. He spent six months with the mission team in East Keswick. During that period, he was engaged to an American girl who also worked for Youth 2000. Realizing he was not called to married life, John broke off the engagement after 18 months. 'I feel my calling is as a lay, single person, working in a secure environment of evangelization', he explains. 'Someone once asked me: "What's the most important thing in your life?" I said: "To bring as many souls as possible to God".'

In September 2001, John left England to work for Youth 2000 in Ireland. Since then, he has travelled the length and breadth of the 26 counties in the Republic of Ireland and throughout Northern Ireland. He has given his testimony hundreds of times in schools, parishes, and on retreats. He prays for three hours a day and whenever he is witnessing to his faith, he is surrounded by a group of three or four people who are praying for him. 'On a parish mission, I might speak to 600 people at a time', he says. 'Last year I was in Derry. I was absolutely exhausted. I'd been giving talks during the day and speaking at parishes in the evening. I said to God: "Does what we're doing make any difference?" Someone then told me there was a lady who wanted to speak to me. The woman came up to me in tears and said: "You visited a school today and gave your testimony to my 15 year-old girl. Two weeks ago, she tried to kill herself. My daughter came home and repeated word for word everything you had said. It took 45 minutes. You had said she could choose life with Jesus or life without him. I'd watched my little girl die when she was 12, when she stopped believing in Christ. Now she's alive again.'"

Another time a 72-year-old man walked up to John and said: 'Thank you for your testimony. Last night I got rid of 48 years of sin. I met Jesus personally in confession.' John adds: 'Both of those incidents happened when I was really down. Yet God always picks me up every time.'

More recently he was lying in bed, praying. 'I was reflecting on my own selfish and lustful desires. I said to Our Lady: "You've really got your work cut out with me". I heard a voice in my heart saying: "If you continue to glorify my Son, he'll make you a saint". I realized I had to hand over my weaknesses to Christ and he would make me holy. I can't do it by myself. All spiritual growth depends on being honest with yourself before God.'

Chapter 6

Clare Ward

CHANGED LIFE

1. NAME: Clare Ward
2. DATE OF BIRTH: May 17th 1973
3. PLACE OF BIRTH: Bromham, near Bedford
4. FAMILY: Youngest of 5 children, lost dad in early childhood
5. EDUCATION: Bedford High School, Manchester University, Trinity and All Saints University College, Leeds
6. TEENAGE AMBITION: To be a journalist
7. CURRENT OCCUPATION: Team member for the Catholic Agency to Support Evangelisation (CASE)
8. TURNING POINT: Giving up her job with the BBC to work for Youth 2000

Clare Ward

It was another hectic day in the newsroom when Clare Ward told her boss she would be leaving her job with the BBC in search of a radical new lifestyle. She was just 26 years old with a promising career in broadcast journalism. In three short years she had risen from a part-time religious affairs correspondent to a news producer. During that time, she had presented the news, travelled the world and reported on Princess Diana's funeral. While most people her age could only dream of a job with the BBC, Clare had it all on a plate. She was successful and her life was secure. New opportunities were constantly opening up and she was all set to keep rapidly climbing the career ladder. Yet deep down she didn't feel fulfilled and wanted something more. She had reached a crossroads in her life and knew that the signpost was pointing in another direction.

Over a period of several months, Clare had realized she was being called to abandon her life to God completely. It gradually became clear that the call meant she had to leave journalism and begin a new journey down an unknown road. 'From a career point of view, I had the world at my feet', reveals Clare. 'I thought of Matthew's Gospel where Jesus says: "If you lose your life for my sake, you will save it". I had lost one life. I'd struggled to let go of it and felt as if I was taking up the cross to boldly persevere down Calvary. Instead of finding a cross, I found immense inner peace.'

Clare was born into a Catholic family in Bromham near Bedford. She was the youngest of five children and the only girl. Her mum was a Lancashire-born Catholic and her dad was Polish. 'My staple diet of growing up was arm wrestling and war games with my brothers', she laughs. 'We lived in an idyllic village and would play out until all hours and go blackberry picking.' Faith played an important role in Clare's family life and Sunday Mass and bedtime prayers were part and parcel of her childhood routine. Her grandmother also lived with the family.

One evening when Clare was six years old, she returned home to find hordes of people swarming round the house. She squeezed through the crowds into the living room, where her dad was lying dead. 'He looked like he was asleep', she recalls. 'His death didn't register. Sometimes I'd ask my mum: "When's Daddy coming back?"' As the years went by, she felt his loss more keenly, particularly when she watched friends being picked up from school by their dads or at significant times of year such as Father's Day. 'I still didn't lack for anything', stresses Clare. 'I didn't have a father figure but I did have four older brothers who looked out for me and a wonderful mum'.

Losing her dad and being brought up in a one-parent family meant she was very close to her mother. 'I saw the sacrifices she made for us and the struggles she had on her own', explains Clare. 'She was also in bad health'.

Her mum was diagnosed with cancer when Clare was just 11 years old. Round about the same time her grandmother suffered a stroke and eventually died. Her mum began intensive radiotherapy treatment, and for a time Clare had to board at school and live with relatives during the holidays. 'It was an unsettling few years', she recalls. 'I remember I hadn't seen my mum for a couple of months. One day she came to school at playtime and she looked like a skeleton. I sat on her lap and cried. By God's grace I was surrounded by loving people. I can't praise the school and head teacher enough for their support and care. It was a very painful time but I always had a sense of being so loved that there was never despair. From my earliest days, I have had a loving relationship with the most loving person in the world – Jesus.'

With no husband and five children, Clare's mum bravely battled against cancer. During her illness, she made a pilgrimage to Lourdes. 'People thought she was going to die', says Clare. 'The first round of treatment didn't work'. Clare and her mum were invited on a parish trip to Medjugorje. 'Mum got the privilege of going inside the room of the apparitions. I was outside and was conscious of the presence of Our Lady. It was like a gentle breeze. I knew in my heart that Our Lady had come as a mother to me. It was the first time I'd felt Our Lady's spiritual motherhood. From that moment on, I never doubted the message of Medjugorje. I prayed for my mum and I asked Our Lady to help. When we returned home, Mum had more treatment and made a full recovery. I really believed that, through the intercession of Our Lady, God had helped my family.'

In the years that followed, Clare settled down to her studies and her mum was able to return to her job as a teacher. Unlike many of her peers, she did not go through a teenage rebellion. 'So much had gone on in my life', she explains. 'What was there to rebel against? If you lose people close to you early in life, you have a different outlook and tend to treasure moments. Having nearly lost my mum, I wasn't in a rush to push her away.'

Clare sat A levels in theology, English literature, economics and politics. She began studying English and linguistics at Manchester University in 1991 but left after a few weeks because she hated the course. She took a gap year and worked as a tour guide for a pilgrimage company. She accompanied pilgrims around Lourdes, showing them St Bernadette's home and other important sites. 'It was an immense time of grace, being in such a beautiful place. People would arrive with the worries of the world but, through prayer and by the grace of God, they would be utterly transformed by the end of the week.'

By now, Clare was also involved with Youth 2000 and had attended several retreats. She was present in Medjugorje during the 1990 youth festival and had picked up a leaflet about UK events. 'Through Youth 2000 I came to a much deeper understanding of how Jesus loved me personally', she reveals. 'It was so awesome to see young people in love with the Blessed Sacrament. After my first retreat I came away thinking I'd just spent the weekend in heaven with the saints', she chuckles. 'It was such a profound experience. I'd never experienced anything like it anywhere else.'

Clare returned to Manchester University after her gap year to study theology and religious studies. She joined a weekly parish prayer group and continued to attend Youth 2000 retreats on a regular basis. But her time at university marked the beginning of a new struggle. Away from home for the first time, she experienced what she describes as a 'delayed adolescence' that lasted for several months. She explains: 'I had a crisis which had started to develop during my final year at school. I really felt as if I was in the utter, deepest pits, like being in hell. Before, things that caused pain had come from the outside. This was happening inside. I remember one night in particular in a nightclub thinking to myself very consciously: "The only reason I'm in this place is to take away the pain".'

During this dark period, Clare questioned her very existence. She also admits that she made a lot of mistakes. 'I did things in total weakness and poverty', she says. 'It was a real experience of coming to terms with the past, understanding the present and being hopeful about the future. The only thing that brought me out of it was finding my identity in Christ. He was the only one that made sense and he drew me out of this abyss. I was also helped by being a member of a prayer group and having close friends. Even when you're following Christ, you still have to make the choice to love yourself and others, or not. God has been increasingly merciful to me. If I didn't know his forgiveness, I wouldn't be able to follow Christ. Even when you follow him, the battle continues to choose life or death. Thankfully God keeps forgiving. Life doesn't become perfect because you convert. It gives you the perseverance and hope to keep trying.'

In difficult moments, Clare would flip open the Bible for inspiration. She would often land on a key passage of Scripture such as 'I am the way, the truth and the life' (John 14:6). She also made a point of having a quiet time with Jesus, present in the Blessed Sacrament. Her faith continued to grow, and she was now preparing for a career in journalism. While she was studying for her degree, Clare worked for hospital radio and on a Sunday morning religious programme for BBC Radio GMR in Manchester. She also freelanced for Catholic newspapers and took part in a Radio 1 pilot programme, Believer Bating, where young people thrashed out ideas about their beliefs.

After graduating in 1995, she began a Master's degree in bimedia journalism at Trinity and All Saints College, Leeds. At the end of the course, she started to work for BBC Radio Leeds. For 18 months, she was a religious affairs reporter before moving into the newsroom full time and covered anything from murders and fires to dog 'singing' competitions.

'It was a hard environment', says Clare. 'There's no place in a newsroom for people who can't hack it'. Colleagues respected her beliefs but, if Clare was asked for her opinion on an issue, she would always give it. 'I remember one day doing a story about adoption for gay couples', she recalls. 'There were gay people in the newsroom and they expected me to approach the story in a bigoted way. I knew that as a BBC journalist I had to be impartial and give both sides of the story. My gay colleagues congratulated me afterwards. The way you approach these stories as a Christian is important. You may not agree with an issue but you can still do it in a loving, truthful, compassionate and non-judgemental way.'

Another time, on Ash Wednesday, Clare had been to Mass in her lunch hour and received the ashes. Back at work, colleagues kept commenting on the dirty mark on her head. She laughs: 'After the sixth person had come up to me, someone shouted out: "It's Ash Wednesday, that's why Clare's got a mark on her head". It was a small way I could witness to my faith.'

The opportunity to witness and share with others sometimes came in the shape of work assignments. On one occasion, she travelled to the Caribbean with a Bradford rabbi to make a documentary about his ministry to Jewish people on cruise ships.

Clare loved her job but in 1999 she realized it had changed her. 'I was becoming a person I didn't like or recognize', she says. 'This doesn't happen to every journalist, but I was becoming so caught up in work and career that my job was taking over my entire life. I was repeatedly cancelling arrangements with friends because of work. Sometimes I didn't see my family for months. I was starting to become a bit cynical. At times I had inflated stories and this worried me. I also began to miss Mass for work. It was clear that there were wonderful career opportunities ahead of me. I could look forward to a good salary, house and a car but I felt this path would lead me away from God.' Rather than risk this, Clare decided to give everything up to follow Jesus, just like the twelve apostles.

Before making her final decision, Clare made a 30 day consecration to Our Lady to ask for her help. 'It enabled me to hand over my life to Jesus in a deeper way', she reveals. 'I made the consecration for guidance on whether I should carry on in the world, so to speak, or do something which would appear totally crazy in most people's eyes. It became clear at the end of it that I had to leave journalism and totally surrender my life to God. At the time Youth 2000 needed help running the national office. I was offered accommodation in the guest room of a Carmelite monastery nearby. I was on cloud nine.'

Although Clare knew she had made the right choice, she was 'terrified' about telling people about her decision. 'I knew in the world's eyes it would appear totally ridiculous. There were people queuing up for jobs with the BBC. I told my boss. He was a Christian and was very understanding and gracious.'

But she still dreaded her colleagues' reaction. 'I expected rejection and imagined people would say I'd gone off my trolley. I was astounded when a number of non-Christians came up to me and offered their support. One said: "I really admire you. I wish I had the courage to follow my heart but I love money too much." I felt my decision had touched some people at the deepest level of their beings. Thanks to God's grace, I was able to respond to my deepest desire. The only

person in life who could help me respond to my deepest desire
was Jesus Christ.'

For the next 18 months, Clare was a full-time volunteer for
Youth 2000. She worked alongside John Pridmore (Chapter 5)
and Niall Slattery, who was involved in football violence,
drink and drugs before his conversion. 'We were totally on
fire with the gospel', says Clare. Half a year into the work,
three other young women joined Clare on the Youth 2000
mission team.

'As a foursome, we decided we'd go to every single diocese
in the country and visit schools. We finished the year on our
knees – literally. It was 2000, the Jubilee year, but there was
no better way we could have spent it.' The experience led
Clare into an even deeper relationship with God. 'Once
you've completely and radically handed everything over to
God, you can't live any other way. It never ceases to be the
most satisfying adventure. Journalism gave me a sense of
adventure but it could never match the adventure of following
Jesus. It's body, heart, mind and soul. It's the full package.'

In 2001, after an immensely powerful experience at the heart
of Youth 2000, Clare felt called to a more permanent way of
life. She was drawn to the Community of the Beatitudes in

Normandy. This lay community is made up of people from all walks of life: families, single people and consecrated brothers and sisters. The consecrated members make a personal consecration, or private vows, to Jesus to be celibate and live a life totally committed to him, alongside families. 'I felt that this was where God wanted me to go', says Clare. 'The call to a celibate vocation is like falling in love and then reaching a point where you know that the person is for you. For me, Jesus was that person.'

Clare spent nearly two years in France with the Beatitudes. 'I learnt a lot about myself. It was a time of going into the desert to grow. After a few years of hectic activity, God had called me away from family, friends and Youth 2000. It was a time of formation. It was also difficult. It meant challenges, tolerance, giving and asking for forgiveness. I learnt what it really was to have a forgiving heart and to be forgiven. At the heart of any family community is the art of loving and forgiving. When the going gets tough in today's society, people often choose to end relationships and go their separate ways. The Christian call is to stay and persevere. This is how we grow.'

In January 2003, Clare was being led once again in a new direction. She felt compelled to return to England and work as a missionary. She now realized her calling wasn't to make a lifelong commitment to a lay community. She put the decision before God in prayer. She went to the chapel and opened the Bible on a passage which said: 'Go and do all that is in your heart. The Lord is with you'. Clare explains: 'The Word of God is alive and active. God can speak powerfully to people through the Bible. I've often asked for direction at times when I've needed a direct answer. The Church tells us God speaks to us through people and events and, very importantly, through the Word of God. This is why the Bible is such an important authority.'

Back in England, Clare returned to Youth 2000 to test her vocation to missionary work. She helped set up a school of evangelization and formation for young people in Leeds. Later that year, she was sent a job advert for a post with a new church evangelization agency. 'Various people had sent me job adverts, but most had bored me silly. Whereas other ads went in the bin, this one lit a fire, so I applied. Even so, I didn't think I had much of a chance. It was London-based, and I'd been out of the country for two years. I was really shocked when I was called to interview. The day of the interview was a nightmare. My train was late. By the time I arrived, the sweat was dripping off me. I found the interview tough. I had to give a presentation and face questions from a panel.'

Clare was offered a job with the Catholic Agency to Support Evangelization, CASE, a new body with a remit to support and resource the Church in England and Wales in the task of evangelization. She took up the post in September 2003 and works alongside two priests and another lay person in equipping dioceses throughout England and Wales for evangelization. 'Many people hear the word "evangelization" and are terrified by it', says Clare. 'They imagine people on soapboxes or knocking on doors, saying: "Turn or burn". Our office is saying "evangelization" isn't a word to be frightened of. It's far more positive and holistic and is not exclusively about preaching. It's about a total way of life. It's about being in an evangelizing family, sharing our faith with our neighbours and friends. It's about sending religious Christmas cards and sharing feast days.'

She adds: 'I'm increasingly passionate about the gospel. God has done so much in my own life to literally save me. I know there are other people who want and need to hear the things God has on offer for them. My life is totally surrendered to this task and through my work, I hope I can play a small part in helping others to be confident about sharing the good news of God's wonderful mercy and love.'

For more information on the Catholic faith or evangelization, please visit www.caseresources.org.uk and www.lifeseekers.co.uk

Chapter 7
Martin Foley

CHANGED LIFE

Martin Foley

1. NAME: Martin Foley
2. DATE OF BIRTH: August 31st 1973
3. PLACE OF BIRTH: Walmley, Birmingham
4. FAMILY: 2nd of 3 children
5. EDUCATION: Bishop Walsh Secondary School, Sutton Coldfield, Manchester University
6. TEENAGE AMBITION: To be a lawyer
7. CURRENT OCCUPATION: Clerk to the All-Party Parliamentary Pro-Life Group
8. TURNING POINT: Moving to London to work in Parliament

Martin Foley looked up from his desk to find one of the senior partners from the law firm angrily waving a pile of papers. 'This is crap', she shouted across the office. 'You really have to buck your ideas up, Martin, if you want to be a solicitor'. She threw down the papers on to his desk and stormed off. Martin could feel his colleagues' eyes boring into him. Humiliated, he didn't know where to look. He had a sinking feeling in the pit of his stomach, unable to understand what he was doing wrong. His work had never been criticized like this either at school or university. He was used to getting on in life and had never before felt so demoralized.

His confidence knocked, Martin tried to pick himself up and press on with his work. Another partner sent him on an errand to the County Court in Birmingham. It was a beautiful summer's day, but Martin sat miserably on the train. He was seriously wondering whether he should go back to the law firm and carry on with his training contract. As he walked around the city in desperation he wondered whether he should jack in his job. But if he did, he wouldn't qualify as a solicitor. He was facing a desperate choice.

Martin grew up in a close-knit Irish Catholic family in the Sutton Coldfield area of Birmingham. He had a happy childhood and would play football for endless hours in the summer with a group of school friends. Throughout his formative years, his parents' strong faith and marriage provided a stable environment. Family prayer and Sunday Mass were an integral part of his life. 'My mum and dad also prayed together daily', recalls Martin. 'They'd talk to us about guardian angels and the saints. I knew I was named after St Martin of Porres.'

Outside the home Martin's parents were active in the local Catholic community, where his dad was a Eucharistic minister, a covenant agent and a member of the parish council. His mum helped out at the local Life house, which provided support for pregnant women in crisis. 'Her involvement there had a big influence on my eventual choice of career', says Martin. 'I remember helping to paint a Life house in Edgbaston that would provide accommodation for women facing crisis pregnancies. At school a number of teachers talked to us about pro-life issues. I was struck by the injustice of abortion and knew this was an area I wanted to tackle in later life.'

In the early 1980s, Martin's family was hit by the recession. His dad was made redundant from his job of 28 years. After that his dad struggled to hold down a permanent job and in 1985 he had a heart bypass operation. At school Martin worked hard and decided he would like to be a solicitor. In

1991 he sat A levels in religious studies, politics, history and general studies. The same year he was offered a place to study law at Manchester University. During freshers' week, he discovered there was a pro-life society run by final year medical students. 'I noticed they were very trendy and didn't fit my pre-conceived notion of what pro-lifers were like', he explains. 'So I signed up. In my second year they asked me to stand for a post on the student union council for the law faculty. I stood on a pro-life ticket against a Jewish guy and won. Afterwards I went to a few meetings but they were very politicized. The Jewish and Islamic societies were at each other's throats. We spent significant periods of time trying to solve the problems of the Middle East.'

Martin took his studies seriously but never really settled into Manchester's student environment. Neither heavy drinking nor clubbing were his scene. He broke his leg twice playing football and missed his friends from home. 'A large group of friends had gone to Leeds, and I really missed the camaraderie. We were all cradle Catholics and were really close.'

But Martin noticed that some of his peers had drifted away from their faith. Many had become atheists or agnostics in their late teens. Others had become involved with sex. 'I found that difficult', reveals Martin. 'I still went to Mass but I felt set apart. It put up a barrier.'

At university, Martin kept up his practice of going to Mass and at times struggled with his faith. 'I always felt that the Church's teaching was fundamentally right', he explains. 'I always believed it. It was part and parcel of my life and part of my identity. I didn't pray regularly or with any particular pattern but I always liked going into a church and praying in front of the Blessed Sacrament. I just hung in there.'

After graduating in 1994, Martin went to law school in Birmingham. The following year he began training to be a solicitor at a firm in Walsall, West Midlands. Martin found the work tedious and, despite his best efforts, often landed himself in trouble. On the day he came close to resigning from his job, he had reached a really low ebb. He felt lonely and worried about the future. He was keen to get married one day but he didn't even have a girlfriend. Neither were there any girls on the horizon. All he had was a job he didn't like. He wanted to walk away but felt it would be the wrong decision. Whatever the future held, he was determined at least to finish his training contract. The sharp words of a disgruntled partner would not stand in the way of his career.

Martin qualified as a solicitor in 1998. In the meantime, his dad's health had started to decline. Things took a turn for the worse when his dad woke up one night with chest pains. It was December 1999, and Martin's mum rushed into his room, asking him to call an ambulance. Shortly after arriving at the hospital, his dad had a massive heart attack and died. His death was a painful and sad time for the family. Martin's faith helped him through the trauma of losing his dad. 'My faith gave me hope', he reveals. 'I never felt angry with God. I felt thankful for my dad and everything he'd done for me. There were no bad memories. We'd never fallen out with each other. We were very close.'

Martin was still disillusioned with his work as a solicitor. The following year he gave up his job to do a Master's degree in health care ethics and law. He returned to Manchester University for a year's postgraduate study and faced a whole new set of challenges. 'Most of the lectures were pro-abortion, pro-euthanasia and pro-infanticide or just plain wishy-washy', he recalls. 'I was forced to confront what I really believed in'. His lecturers were not in sympathy with his pro-life views and would strongly challenge his arguments. 'The course really stimulated me', says Martin. It also changed the direction of his career.

Encouraged by his mum, Martin wrote to Lord Alton, a leading Catholic peer, for advice. Martin had always been interested in politics and had followed Lord Alton's career in politics from when he was an MP in the House of Commons. He was amazed when Lord Alton phoned him and invited him to a meeting in Liverpool. 'We spent three hours talking about pro-life issues and politics', recalls Martin. 'Halfway through the conversation, Lord Alton turned to me and said: "Would you like to come and work for me in Parliament?"'

Martin moved to London in September 2001, after completing his Master's degree. Aged 28 he began work as Lord Alton's assistant. The work covered a range of pro-life and human rights issues and was the perfect grounding for his new career in politics. The following summer, Martin was asked if he would like to work alongside Jim Dobbin, the Labour MP for Heywood and Middleton. He was offered the post of clerk to the All-Party Parliamentary Pro-Life Group. Martin also started going into schools to talk about pro-life issues and to empower young people to make a difference.

'I once went to a Catholic sixth form and the debate moved on to whether it's legitimate to have an abortion after being raped', says Martin. 'I talked about the issue from a human rights perspective and explained why we're all entitled to the right to life from the moment of conception, regardless of the circumstances of our conception. Rape is a very, very rare case. I asked the young people to consider whether they believed the rapist should be given a lethal injection and if he should be denied his right to life.

'I am opposed to capital punishment, but the liberal elite would be up in arms about the idea of condemning a rapist to death. Yet this has been the fate of more than five million unborn babies since abortion was legalized in this country. Most young people I talk to have not yet made up their minds on these issues but they're very influenced by what the media says. I often compare abortion to slavery. In the same way people once believed slavery was part and parcel of life, despite the injustice of it, abortion has become acceptable in today's society, and unborn children continue to die. I try to get young people to think in a less utilitarian way. Instead of approaching life in terms of what makes them happy or sad, I ask them to put aside the consequences and consider if having an abortion is right or wrong. I also tell students what an abortion involves from a physical and psychological perspective and describe the development of the foetus.'

In January 2002 Martin encountered Youth 2000 for the first time. Little did he realize it would change the course of his life. He started to attend a Youth 2000 prayer group in London where young people gathered together every week. He was amazed at what he witnessed. 'I saw young people praying the rosary', he says. 'It was an incredibly moving experience. They were normal young people with problems and careers just like me. But their faith was part of their life.'

Martin developed deep friendships with many of those in the group. One of his new friends was Anna-Marie, a young doctor, who had been attending Youth 2000 prayer groups and retreats since the age of sixteen. There was an instant attraction between them, but Martin was too shy to ask her out. At the time Anna-Marie was seeing someone else. It was some time later when Martin discovered that, within weeks of meeting him, she was convinced he was the man she would marry.

Anna-Marie came from a family of converts, and Martin was fascinated by her unusual background. Her grandfather was the German economist Ernest Fritz Schumacher, author of *Small is Beautiful*. He had approached his faith from an intellectual point of view. He had first been attracted to Buddhism but gradually realized his spirituality was better suited to Christianity. His daughter and Anna-Marie's mum, Barbara, had already become a Catholic, and was instrumental in Schumacher's conversion to Catholicism. She has published her own book about him entitled *Alias Papa*. Anna-

Marie's dad, Don, a former Anglican, has also embraced the Catholic faith.

Anna-Marie is one of six children. Following a pilgrimage to Medjugorje with her mum, she started attending a Youth 2000 prayer group in South Kensington. After taking her A levels she worked for six months in India and then studied medicine at Bristol University. She is now a GP.

Martin fell in love with Anna-Marie and seized opportunities to see her outside the prayer group in the presence of friends. The members of the group would often go to the pub together after their weekly meeting. Martin and Anna-Marie would usually end up locked in conversation. They also visited Kew Gardens with friends but spent the day walking alone together. 'I found Anna-Marie very attractive', reveals Martin. 'I was desperate to say something but I was too shy. In the end I didn't know what to say. Eventually, we started to email and text each other.'

The turning point came after Martin and Anna-Marie both decided to apply to join the same Augustinian lay community in Hammersmith. The community required members to be single. There was also a strict ban on dating within the community. 'I was first to be interviewed by two priests for the community in June 2002', recalls Martin. 'During the interview, I was asked: "Is there anything stopping you from joining this community?" I stammered: "Well, there's this girl I like and she's going to join too". After that, I knew they'd never offer me a place.'

As Martin left the interview, a text message arrived from Anna-Marie. 'I was still slightly unsure of her intentions and I was really worried that she would join the community.' Anna-Marie had her interview and was offered a place but turned it down. Her decision gave Martin the impetus he needed to ask her out. 'Our first date was on 5 July 2002', recalls Martin, tenderly. 'We went to Mass together at Westminster Cathedral. I walked Anna-Marie home and kissed her for the first time.'

Anna-Marie told him how she had always hoped to meet someone who shared her faith. Martin suggested they pray together. From that moment on, they would pray together each time they met. They got engaged on 22 August 2003 and married at Our Lady of Loreto and St Winefride's Church in Kew, Richmond, on 3 January 2004. Anna-Marie gave birth to twins, Catherine Therese and Joseph, later that year on 19 October.

Prayer continues to be at the heart of their relationship. As a married couple, Martin and Anna-Marie pray together every morning and evening. They describe the experience as 'the glue that keeps them together' through good times and bad. It is a discipline that gives them great strength. 'If we weren't praying together, we wouldn't be sharing as much as we could', says Martin. 'We share the same hopes for a successful marriage. We've both been through stressful times at work and have had to help each other through difficulties. It has been a great source of unity and helped us to solve problems peacefully.'

Chapter 8
Sister Catherine

CHANGED LIFE

1. **NAME:** Sister Catherine
2. **DATE OF BIRTH:** May 26th 1982
3. **PLACE OF BIRTH:** Cambridge
4. **FAMILY:** Oldest of 5 children
5. **EDUCATION:** Home-schooled
6. **TEENAGE AMBITION:** To be a doctor
7. **CURRENT OCCUPATION:** A contemplative nun
8. **TURNING POINT:** Turning down a place at medical school

Sister Catherine

In the eyes of the world Catherine Underwood threw away her career on the day she gave up her place at medical school to enter a convent. Aged 19 with excellent qualifications, her future success was all but guaranteed. Yet she still chose to sacrifice a promising medical career to be a contemplative nun. Undoubtedly there were those who thought her decision was an act of madness. What would happen if she changed her mind? By turning her back on medicine, she may have damaged her prospects, even ruined her life.

When Catherine entered Tyburn Convent in London on 1 November 2001, the feast of All Saints, she made an act of faith not easily understood in today's world. Her decision was a moment of great joy because she knew in her heart that the Lord Jesus was calling her to a contemplative way of life. As a Benedictine nun her life would be structured around prayer, work and study. She would swap her comfortable bedroom at home for a simple convent cell. She would renounce all her property. The clothes she was wearing would be put away. She would only see her family once a month when they came to visit. It was the beginning of a new life that involved sacrifices, but she was ready to embrace it wholeheartedly.

Catherine realized she had a vocation to religious life at an early age. 'I was so young that I can't put an age on it', she says. 'I wondered if I was just attracted to an image of a nun but, if I went on retreats, there were key times when I knew it was a real possibility for the future'. She grew up in Cambridge, where her dad worked at St John's College as an archivist. For most of her life, she and her younger sisters, Lucy and Margaret, were home-schooled by her mum. Her brother, John, and youngest sister, Rosemary, are twins and are still taught at home.

For Catherine's parents, passing on the Catholic faith to their children was their number one priority in life. 'Practising the faith was more than going to Mass and church', she explains. 'My parents took us to Mass every Sunday but also in the week. Our faith was part of our home life. We kept the liturgical year and celebrated the feast days. Each of us had a special feast day. Mine was the feast of St Catherine of Siena on 29 April. On our feast day, we would receive a card and a little present. It would be a religious present like a book on the saint's life. We would also light our baptismal candle. My father had painted mine, and it was almost burnt out by the time I left home. On our feast day we would also go to Mass. The high festivals were always celebrated within the home. On Christmas Eve, we would have a little ceremony next to the crib'.

Catherine attended her local Catholic primary school for three years before her parents decided to home-school. 'I remember the day my mother said to us: "Would you like not to have to go to school any more?" I was really happy, because school took many hours out of every day. I remember a lot of things going on inside me that I couldn't express at that age. For example, being with a huge group of children, particularly at the age of four and five, was hard. I came from a happy home environment to this artificial environment that was school. There were children there with problems such as aggression in the playground. I remember being quite sucked into the idea that there were certain characters in the class that one had to imitate or be liked by to get on at school.'

When she was old enough to understand, Catherine's parents explained the reasons behind their decision to home-school. 'One of the main reasons was to protect our own faith and integrity. My parents were also concerned that our gifts and talents could be crushed by the school system.'

Her parents took great pains to make sure that Catherine and her siblings participated in a wide range of extracurricular activities where they could socialize with other children. She went to dance school, played the violin in an orchestra and took part in sports courses. 'I had some very close teenage friends', she recalls. 'I became more and more aware that I was not doing the same things as my teenage peers. I didn't have a desire to go out late or experiment with drinking. I remember some of the youngsters in the dancing school were experimenting with shoplifting. I was scandalized. I realized there were terrible influences in society and that the TV programmes and teen magazines were full of sex and violence. The conversation could sometimes turn unpleasant.'

She explains: 'I remember that many of them were fascinated by home-schooling and I was fascinated by school. I was curious to know what happened in school and what their day was like. They were curious to know what I did at home. Some of them admired me for being a bit different.'

Naturally there were times when she did wonder how her life would have turned out if she had not been home-schooled. 'I wondered where I would have been in the social scene. 'When the time came to prepare for my GCSEs, I wondered if it might be better to go to school'. Instead, she stayed at home, sat her first three GCSEs at the age of 14 and managed an A grade in German, and Bs in English language and mathematics. She took another six later on, achieving As and Bs in all of her subjects apart from a C in biology.

She was now at an age where her peers were becoming involved in relationships with the opposite sex. Catherine remembers being bored by 'boy talk' and the accompanying tales of unrequited love and heartbreak. 'I never felt that the experiences described were very genuine', she says. 'It wasn't real romance. It was coming out of magazines. Some of my peers said they were involved in relationships. The way we talked about it at home was much more healthy. I saw everything in terms of vocation. We talked about how having a relationship with a man was a beautiful part of growing up and being a woman. It was a different world for me. The kind of relationship my parents would have been happy for me to have would have been a friendship. For the other girls, it was all geared towards putting into practice the information that they'd got from school and copying the heros and heroines from the soap operas. It all went over my head.'

Despite the gulf between her own experience and that of her teenage peers, Catherine felt a genuine affection for many of the girls she knew from the dance school and the orchestra. 'I had many happy conversations with them. When we did performances at dance school, I had a wonderful time. With hindsight, I wish I'd been stronger and witnessed to my own faith and values.'

Catherine started attending daily Mass at the age of 12 when she was preparing for her confirmation. 'The Mass gave me the grace I needed to help me not to be led astray', she reveals.

'There were temptations. I felt the allurement of fashion and I wanted to be popular with my friends. At home I was safe and I could display my strengths. Outside the home environment I didn't think my gifts would be valued as much. My knowledge of my faith prevented me from living a double life.'

After her GCSEs, Catherine started to consider seriously what she should do with her life. The possibility of a religious vocation was still at the back of her mind, but she was also attracted to a career in medicine. She decided to study sciences and maths at A level. It was a big step, because the specialist knowledge required meant it would be better for her to study for A levels at her local sixth form college. Both she and her teachers had concerns about how she would cope. 'I went there not knowing what to expect', says Catherine. 'I threw myself into it. I was determined to work hard and do well academically. College provided a mature environment, because everyone who was there had chosen to be there. All the teachers were amazed that I managed to settle in so well. The teachers had made it clear that they were worried when I started college. In the end they were astounded and said it wasn't obvious that I hadn't been to school first.'

Going to college also opened the door to a whole new set of friends and experiences. 'I got on well in class', says

Catherine. 'I had a group of friends. I remember I enjoyed being with some groups more than others. I saw my time at college as an opportunity to witness to my faith. Again I wish I'd been stronger. There was a sense of wanting something better for the young people around me. I wanted everyone of them to have a sense of vocation and know the love of God. At that time, I was becoming more and more aware of the culture of death. The pro-life issue was at the forefront of my mind. I saw that human life was under threat. I had many excellent discussions on that issue with my friends and in class. At sixth form college I woke up to how young people were being led astray.'

Some of her friends started to go clubbing, but she was not convinced they really enjoyed it. Catherine went to parties and enjoyed herself without becoming involved in heavy drinking or drugs. 'I always kept in mind the sound words of advice my mother had given me', she explains. 'I was able to make discerning decisions, and my mother was able to trust my decisions. This was one of the things my mum had hoped for in taking us out of school.'

Outside college, Catherine became involved in Youth 2000. She had made a number of Catholic friends through the National Association of Catholic Families. One of her friends was Emilia Klepacka. 'Emilia had spoken very highly of

Youth 2000', she recalls. 'There was also a religious sister, a Dominican, and she invited me to come on a retreat with her'. Catherine and her younger sister, Lucy, attended the Youth 2000 millennium festival at Liverpool Metropolitan Cathedral at the end of 1999. 'I was bowled over by the vibrant faith of the young people there, the testimonies and the conversions. There were so many people who had become depressed and whose lives had become aimless; they had turned to all sorts of things to find a way out, such as drugs, drinking and crime. Now they were so full of joy and had realized they would only be totally happy by turning to God. It was so beautiful. It was like witnessing the manifestation of God's love for all these people. It increased my own faith in the power of God in a person's life. In Liverpool what struck me most was the zeal for evangelization. I remember we were all sent out to Liverpool city centre to invite people to the all-night vigil on New Year's Eve.'

Through Youth 2000 she witnessed a real love of the sacraments of the Church, devotion to Our Lady and a burning desire to spread the gospel. She was also inspired by the self-sacrificing faith of the leaders and the mission team. 'These were people who had made spreading the gospel their number one priority', she says. 'Everyone had their different gifts. In Youth 2000 you could really see people's gifts being used for God's glory. Young people discovered they had talents they never knew. No one was left in any doubt that each person is called to grow in holiness.'

Once, at a small retreat, Catherine felt moved to give her own testimony. Hers was in stark contrast to many of those she would hear. 'Most young people who got up to give their testimonies did so because they'd had terrible struggles in life. They'd been drawn into awful situations and their testimonies were about finding an alternative. Having been so protected by my family, I hadn't experienced the same difficulties and temptations. But I did see that God uses each of us in different ways. Each one of us is called to conversion.'

Catherine also realized that her call to religious life had become more urgent. Throughout her life, there had been times when she had pushed it aside and assumed she would take the career path. She had also wanted to prove to herself that she could succeed in the world before making a final decision.

'What Youth 2000 did for me was to put Christ in the centre and really strengthen my faith in providence and my desire to co-operate with the divine plan', she reveals. 'I had a growing awareness that God's plans for each one of us are more infinitely worthwhile than anything we can think up for ourselves.'

Catherine sat her A levels during the summer of 2000, achieving As in chemistry and biology and a B in maths. She had accepted a place to study medicine at London University but decided to take a gap year before starting her degree.

She was present at World Youth Day in Rome that year. Afterwards she organized a reunion with the group she had met there. The group did a pilgrimage from Westminster to Tyburn Convent in Marble Arch. 'We visited the crypt of the Tyburn martyrs, had a talk and tea with the sisters', says Catherine. 'I noticed that some of the sisters were young. They were Benedictines. I had always been attracted to their way of life. I had previously seen an advert in a paper about them, which had said: "Are you called to a life of divine service and perpetual adoration?" At first I thought: "No I don't think I am". Then I realized that I was very drawn to the idea of perpetual adoration, and that the Mass was the central point of the way of life. I had been discovering the importance of the Mass more and more through Youth 2000. One of the big things I'd learnt through Youth 2000 was the way adoration flows from the Mass. I felt that God was calling me to live a life that is centred on the Mass in a deep and complete way.'

Catherine decided that she now needed to set aside a period of time to discern her vocation. She knew her faith would have to be strong if she were to give up her place at medical school.

In February 2001, she joined the Youth 2000 mission team in East Keswick, near Leeds. For the next six months, Catherine lived and prayed in community and evangelized in schools and parishes. 'We relied so much on each other's prayers when we were speaking in schools. We used to ask the contemplative orders to pray for the success of retreats. On the road, we would pray for the person giving witness. Many people were surprised to hear that I'd gone into an enclosed order after all this witnessing. But I feel there is both an apostolic and contemplative dimension to the Church. I felt that my call was to support the new evangelization through prayer.'

Catherine cancelled her university place shortly before Youth 2000's annual summer prayer festival in Walsingham. On 15 September 2001, the feast of Our Lady of Sorrows, she went to Tyburn Convent for a two-week trial period. During that time, Catherine experienced the contemplative way of life. On a typical day at the convent, the nuns would begin prayers with the divine office at 5.30 a.m. They would also spend two half-hour periods in adoration of the Blessed Sacrament each day and an hour in adoration during the night two or three times a week.

At the end of the trial period, Catherine asked if she could enter the convent and was accepted. She returned to the mission team in East Keswick to say her goodbyes. She also went home to her family to tell them about her decision. 'My family weren't surprised. It was as hard as it would be for any parents when their first daughter leaves home but there was a certain amount of joy and peace that I had found my vocation so young. There was some initial concern that I had given up my place at university, but my parents still supported me. I don't think I'll ever know what really were their fears and doubts.'

Sister Catherine received the habit the following year when she became a novice, in August 2002. At the time of writing this book, she had not yet taken her final vows. She expects to make her monastic profession for life during 2005, when she will receive a white cowl which symbolizes being espoused to Christ. Before she can make her profession, the community of 23 nuns must vote to say they have discerned that she has a vocation to the order.

'By deciding to come here, I was able to put my life in God's hands', says Sister Catherine. 'My life here is about coming to follow Christ more closely. It's also about becoming the person God wants me to be. Community life is about helping each other to come to God by supporting each other. There are both joys and hardships, but it's through living in community that you love and serve your neighbour. When people ask me what I miss about my former life, I genuinely can't think of anything, because I have the joy of knowing that I am doing God's will. He is forming me and bringing me to complete fulfilment in him.'

For more information, please contact:

The Adorers of the Sacred Heart of Jesus of Montmartre,

Tyburn Convent

8 Hyde Park Place

London W2 2LJ

Tel: 0207 723 7262

www.tyburnconvent.org.uk

Chapter 9
Tom Smith

CHANGED LIFE

1. **NAME:** Tom Smith
2. **DATE OF BIRTH:** January 4th 1978
3. **PLACE OF BIRTH:** Salisbury, Wiltshire
4. **FAMILY:** Only child
5. **EDUCATION:** St. Mary's College, Southampton, Manchester University
6. **TEENAGE AMBITION:** To be a rebel
7. **CURRENT OCCUPATION:** Seminarian
8. **TURNING POINT:** Studying abroad

Tom Smith

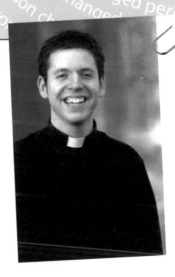

Tom Smith was convinced he had made a terrible mistake on the day he arrived in Holland. His student accommodation was so appalling it reduced him to tears. A cat was on the table in the living room, licking the remains of a filthy saucepan. In the kitchen Tom discovered the most foul, indescribable gunge behind the refrigerator. Yet none of his housemates appeared to care. They all belonged to a student fraternity and spent most of their time drinking. They would try to persuade Tom to join in their rowdy drinking sessions. New members had to pay to join the fraternity. Rituals involved brawls and fights. One year a student was thrown into a canal during his initiation ceremony.

Tom was in Leiden, the Oxford of Holland. It could have been another planet as far as he was concerned. His refusal to get involved with the fraternity left him alienated. Here he was alone in a foreign country, with nowhere to turn. He was engulfed by loneliness, wondering why on earth he had decided to come here.

It was 1997, and Tom was on an Erasmus exchange from his own university back in Manchester. It was the beginning of his second academic year, and he was recovering after the breakdown of a relationship. He had been in love and it hadn't worked out. Now he was trying to broaden his horizons. He was also trying to discover where he really stood in relation to his faith.

Tom came from a practising Catholic family in Salisbury and was baptized into the Catholic Church as a baby. He went to Mass every Sunday. If for any reason his mum couldn't attend, he would be taken to church by his dad, who wasn't a Catholic. 'I remember as a child saying my prayers with my mum before going to sleep. We'd say the Our Father, Hail Mary and Glory Be.' The only time he ever missed Mass was one Christmas when he was staying with relatives. His mum went to an early Mass, and Tom had promised to go to a later service. Instead he lied to his mum, pretending he had been to Mass when he had really slept in. He remembers feeling really pleased that he had missed Mass and got away with it.

Like many boys who were brought up Catholic, Tom became an altar server. As he got older one of his motivations was that it gave him a 'good look at the girls in the congregation'. There was one particular girl that caught his eye. One Sunday he was busy staring at her and accidentally dropped the host at the offertory. He also joined the parish council to try to get closer to her.

Then, when Tom was 14, his parents divorced. From that moment on he was determined to be a rebel. He started to wear hippy clothes and grew his hair long. His headmaster told him to get a haircut. 'I'd cut off a millimetre so next time he challenged me about it I could say I'd got my hair cut.'

He also experimented with cannabis during the long train journey to secondary school in Southampton. 'There was a guy who got on at a station *en route* and I would buy a spliff from him. It wasn't the great experience I was hoping for. He didn't believe in putting much in the spliff. I only tried it about four or five times.'

At the age of 15, Tom started to date girls. 'One girl I went out with was on the pill,' he reveals. 'Being naive, I didn't realize what she wanted. It only came to light two weeks after we broke up, when I found out she was already sleeping with her new boyfriend. My upbringing as a Catholic meant that I wouldn't jump into bed with someone that quickly. I look back now and think that was a real blessing. I knew that the Catholic Church taught that it was wrong to use artificial contraception, so I didn't want to use it, but I hadn't quite linked that with the rest of the Church's teaching on sexuality.'

Tom continued to date girls and would sometimes fall out with his mum over his choice of girlfriends. 'I gave my mum a hard time. I used to slam doors. I felt angry inside. I look back now and of course I see where she was coming from. I remember she once said: "Don't ever bring that girl round again". I used to shout back: "It's my life. I'll bring home whichever girl I want."'

He also remembers being caught on camera at a protest against the extension of the M3 at Twyford Down, Winchester. 'There was a lot of violence going on. I picked up a big fence post and carried it to the protest. Other people were trying to overturn security vehicles with cameras which were taking video footage. Some months later I was watching a documentary with my mum and there I was striding past with a fence post. My mum was really shocked.'

Tom still attended Mass but questioned whether God really existed. Life felt better with God than without, but then there was the whole issue of the Church and all the rules that came with it. One girlfriend lent Tom a book by Kahlil Gibran, the Lebanese poet and philosopher. It was strong on spirituality without rules and explored God through poetry. 'I was searching for a meaning in my life', reveals Tom. 'I'd experimented with cannabis and that had been disappointing'. He had also tried Buddhist meditation, yoga classes and keeping physically fit through running and swimming. For a time he was obsessed with the pop group *Suede*, modelling himself on the lead singer.

When he was 16, one of his teachers took a four-day retreat to Quarr Abbey on the Isle of Wight. Tom was befriended by Father Joe Warrilow, whose guidance would prove invaluable in later years, and he went back to the monastery several times.

'I was struck by the peace of the monastery', says Tom. 'The monks' liturgy was my first experience of contemplative prayer. Even as a teenager who wasn't really into his faith, I had this ideal that simplicity was better than having too many material things. I would often purge my room of things I didn't really need.'

It was during a retreat at the abbey that Tom first became aware of a possible vocation to the priesthood. 'I said to Father Joe: "I want to be like a monk but go out and work with people".' But Tom was scared by the implications of his disclosure and tried to push any further thoughts of priesthood to the back of his mind.

For the moment he had more immediate concerns. He had not been working hard at school and would always leave his revision to the last minute. All of his school reports said he lacked confidence. His A levels were fast approaching and he had not put in nearly enough work. Six months before he sat them he panicked. 'I realized that if I didn't start working I'd fail'. He was relieved when he passed his exams with a B, a C and two Ds. He had the grades he needed for university, but felt disappointed in himself for not having got down to his studies sooner.

In September 1996 Tom left home to study the history of art at Manchester University. 'I saw leaving home as a new opportunity', he says. He remembers being the last student to arrive at the hall of residence. 'All the guys were sitting either side of the corridor, and I had to walk past them all to get to my room. I was really nervous.'

The following morning he turned up at the Catholic chaplaincy at 9 a.m, only to find it locked. 'I thought I could practise my faith freely here', he says. He was so keen to get going he hadn't realized that the student day would not usually get off to such an early start. Tom began to go to Mass every day at the chaplaincy. After Mass the students would have lunch together and there would be opportunities for discussions. He would also attend Mass at the Holy Name Church next to the university, and other churches in the city. He made other friends through the International Society and started dating an Italian girl called Luisa. 'I fell in love with her,' he reveals. 'But things didn't work out then, so we eventually broke up, although we still kept in touch.' Tom decided to apply for an Erasmus exchange to Holland for a term. Little did he know that his time there would send his life off in a whole new direction.

For the first few weeks in Holland, Tom was desperately unhappy. The student fraternity which held gatherings in his house got him down. He had kept in touch with Father Joe at Quarr Abbey and would write to him on a regular basis. During this period his only solace was the Eucharist. On his second day in Leiden Tom went to church. Although he didn't understand a word of the Mass, which was celebrated in Dutch, he felt a wave of reassurance as he received Holy Communion. 'After having had an intense relationship at the end of the first year, it was as if God had taken me away from that environment', he explains. 'I hadn't really involved him in the process but now here I was on my own away from familiar things, and it was here that he spoke to me the loudest'. Tom started going to the university chaplaincy. He also went to St Louis' Church, where Mass was celebrated partly in Latin. 'I felt more at home with the Latin than Dutch', he explains.

Tom was able to go to confession on a regular basis because the parish priest spoke good English and had lived for a while in Dorking, Surrey. He also met two young women, Gemma and Eliza, who had just arrived back from World Youth Day in Paris. Both women were on fire with their faith. Gemma was involved with the Emmanuel Community. Eliza had been a delegate for the Dutch youth at World Youth Day and had met the Pope. Tom started to go to a prayer group run by the community. He went on a pilgrimage to Taizé and a trip to the shrine of Beauraing in the French-speaking part of Belgium. The event was a follow-up to World Youth Day, and the relics of Saint Thérèse of Lisieux were on display. Tom was particularly struck by a talk translated into English by a priest who was the guardian of the shrine of Paray-le-Monial in France. 'He said: "Jesus loves you, Jesus loves you, Jesus loves you". It was his conviction and clarity that impressed me. I remember going home with some other young people from Leiden. I was wearing a cross around my neck and was singing on the train. Gemma was a bit embarrassed. The conviction with which the priest delivered the words "Jesus loves you" had really hit me. Something fundamental had happened.'

Up until this moment Tom felt as if he had been stumbling through his faith without making a real connection with God. When he returned home in December, he wrote the following words in his diary: 'I come back to England with an indescribable enthusiasm to work for the faith in my country'.

In January 1998 Tom returned to university in Manchester and volunteered for work at a drop-in centre for the homeless.

He went back to the chaplaincy to find that the old faces of the previous year had been replaced by new students. He also went on a retreat with the *Verbum Dei* Community on the Isle of Wight. 'It was the first time I'd been on a silent retreat', recalls Tom. 'It brought up so many issues I'd been hiding from, such as anger and negativity that I'd never dealt with properly. It all came to the surface on this silent retreat. It was another turning point and taught me a lot about myself.'

Around Easter that year Tom was put in touch with a priest who worked with young people in Manchester. He was Father Ian Kelly, then the chaplain of Salford University. Father Ian became Tom's spiritual director. He would talk to him about all aspects of the Catholic faith, including the lives of the saints and how each person is called to holiness.

As Tom entered his final year at university, he realized he would soon have to decide on a career and start thinking about job possibilities. He went to the careers office for advice. He was told that if he wanted to combine his degree in the history of art with his faith, then he would have to be like Sr Wendy Beckett, the art critic and nun. Much as he was amused by the careers advice, it was not the solution for which Tom was searching. As the first term was winding up, he was still struggling with a decision.

'In my heart of hearts I knew I wanted to be a priest', he says. 'I told Father Ian that I needed a year of discernment. I didn't want to mention priesthood. He said: "Why, what do you want to discern?" I replied: "I want to discern and pray". He said: "No, pray about what?" I felt as if my back was against the wall. I knew I had to come out with an answer. Then I said in a small voice: "I want to be a priest". I was shuffling uncomfortably in my chair. Father Ian told me I had already discerned my vocation and advised me not to put off my decision any longer.'

When Tom applied for a place at seminary, a childhood memory came flooding back. 'I remembered being about seven years old and attending a funeral', he says. 'I was very aware of the priest's presence. It made a strong impression on me. I realized that, as a priest, I too would be able to bring God's love to people.'

Not long after his application was accepted, Tom was invited to a Youth 2000 retreat by Father Russell Wright, a priest at the Holy Name Church in Manchester. In the past Tom had kept Youth 2000 at arm's length and nicknamed it 'Spoof 2000'. He really didn't know what to expect from the retreat and was greatly relieved to find a peaceful and prayerful atmosphere. 'My abiding memory is of praying in front of the Blessed Sacrament with music playing in the background'.

Tom was so taken by Youth 2000 that he decided to go on two more retreats in quick succession. Later, when he went to seminary, he would often attend retreats during his vacation.

'Youth 2000 gave me a sense of mission', he enthuses. 'It was like God's hand reaching out to grab young people, giving them the opportunity to go to confession and to hear good talks. Witnessing God's love reaching out to young people made me very excited.'

Tom also struck up strong friendships with the young people who lived in a Youth 2000 community in Bow, East London. After his graduation in 1999, Tom joined the community for six weeks in preparation for his priestly training. It was a special time of grace, and each morning the community would worship Jesus through adoration of the Blessed Sacrament.

Tom spent the next two years at seminary in Valladolid in Spain. At first he found his studies in Spanish tough. There were also times when he would question his vocation. 'I found it difficult to settle in and totally embrace my decision to become a priest', he reveals. 'It meant making a commitment. That was frightening at first.'

It also meant ruling out other relationships and marriage. The previous summer Tom had met up with his ex-girlfriend from

Italy, and they continued to write to each other after she went home. At this time he felt that there might be some possibility that they would eventually get back together. 'Part of making the decision to become a priest was having to cancel out relationship possibilities', he says. 'Although it was very difficult, it's a profound thing to choose not to get married for the sake of the kingdom of God'. In 2001 Tom moved to Birmingham to continue his training at Oscott College. He was ordained a deacon on 19 June 2004, the feast of the Immaculate Heart. He made promises of celibacy, respect and obedience to his bishop. He hopes to be ordained a priest in 2005.

'I strongly believe this is God's will for me', he says. 'He wants me as I am and he wants to use me despite all my imperfections. As a priest I hope to be a witness to God's love. I look forward to hearing confessions and helping people out with advice, cleansing them from their sins and being a channel for God's grace. I have experienced many graces and healing through confession. As well as forgiving sins, confession gives us great strength against sin. I'd like others to have this experience too.'

Chapter 10

Robert Toone

CHANGED LIFE

1. NAME: Robert Toone
2. DATE OF BIRTH: August 21st 1968
3. PLACE OF BIRTH: Rotherham, South Yorkshire
4. FAMILY: A twin and the youngest of 5 children
5. EDUCATION: Ampleforth College, York and Cambridge University
6. TEENAGE AMBITION: To be a rich international businessman
7. CURRENT OCCUPATION: Barrister on sabbatical
8. TURNING POINT: Vision of Christ's passion

Robert Toone

It was the perfect picnic on the perfect summer's day. Robert Toone sat lazily in the sunshine, laughing and joking, surrounded by a large group of friends. As the champagne flowed, he felt a glow of satisfaction. The food streamed out of the luxury picnic hamper until he could eat no more. Smoked salmon and strawberries and cream were followed by more champagne. People were dotted here and there painting pictures. It was like a scene from Evelyn Waugh's *Brideshead Revisited*. Robert was entranced. Many in his circle of friends were ridiculously wealthy. The friend who had organized the picnic had a rare car and Robert had enjoyed being driven out to the countryside in it. As he relaxed back on a rug, future success seemed certain. Here he was, an undergraduate at Cambridge University, leading the perfect lifestyle. Or so he thought.

At the end of the day, as the remainder of the food was packed back into the hamper, Robert sat bolt upright. It was a Sunday. He had missed Mass. He insisted that his rich friend drive him back to the Catholic church in Cambridge. There Robert explained to the parish priest how he had come to miss Mass. The priest gave him Holy Communion, and Robert went home. The incident was a warning to him. If he carried on following his superficial desires, he was going to end up very far from his faith.

Ambitious and talented, Robert had his life mapped out long before he took up his place at Cambridge University. All his plans revolved around money, fast cars and foreign travel. He was prepared to sacrifice everything to achieve his dreams. In his gap year between school at Ampleforth, near York, and university, he went first to Paris to learn to speak French fluently and then to Chile to master Spanish. Like many young people of his age, he strove to be in control of his life and wanted to be liked and respected by his peers.

It was Autumn 1987 and he had just turned 19. 'I would be up at 5.30 in the morning to go rowing', he recalls. 'I was also acting, singing in a choir and playing in an orchestra. I was like a live wire. My days were filled with activity. I enjoyed myself but I wasn't really happy. I was trying to fill a hole inside.'

He was slowly drifting away from the Catholic faith instilled in him first by his Irish mother and later by the monks of Ampleforth Abbey. During his first term at Cambridge, Robert was invited to go on pilgrimage by an old school friend to Medjugorje, in the former Yugoslavia. But he turned down the invitation, deciding he had better things to do with his time. Nevertheless, he began to feel drawn to Medjugorje. His mum gave him a book to read about the apparitions said to be taking place there. He also watched a video that featured a young

Irishwoman, Ann Marie. In it she spoke movingly about her younger brother, who had died in a tragic accident whilst on pilgrimage there. 'When I heard her testimony and saw how profound her faith was, I couldn't help but feel moved', reveals Robert.

Ann Marie, who eventually married one of Robert's closest friends, Rod Isaacs (Chapter 3), made a strong impression on Robert. The following summer, during his university holidays, Robert was travelling around Europe in a battered Renault 4 with a group of friends when he decided to go to Medjugorje. As they travelled through France, he was re-reading the Narnia books by C.S. Lewis. They crossed the border into northern Italy, where they were going to stay in a house lent by the parents of one of Robert's friends. Soon after they arrived, an argument broke out about abortion. 'I think some of the group had been affected by abortion so it was an emotional thing', recalls Robert. 'I said I was off to Medjugorje, and everyone laughed at me. But as I was leaving, the guy I'd had the argument with said: "Pray for me".'

Robert left with little idea of how to get to Medjugorje. He headed to Assisi by train and bumped into a girl who played in the same orchestra as him in Cambridge. He was surprised by the unexpected meeting, which marked the beginning of a set of coincidences. He stayed the night in a youth hostel in Assisi and got talking to a group of young people there. When Robert explained he was on his way to Medjugorje, their faces lit up. It reminded him of the description of the radiant faces of Aslan's followers in the Narnia chronicles. It was a sign to Robert that God was taking charge of the situation.

A young man from the hostel decided he would travel with Robert to Medjugorje. They both got up at dawn and slept at the quayside until the first coach of the day pulled in. The very first bus that arrived was going direct to the shrine. Robert and his new friend hitched a lift. Robert was amazed that the bus happened to be a pilgrimage coach. At the time, Medjugorje was still part of Yugoslavia, run by a Communist government hostile to the Catholic faith. So the chances of a pilgrimage coach passing through at exactly the right time were remote.

Once he arrived in Medjugorje, another surprise was in store for Robert. The first person he met was the best friend of Ann Marie, the young woman on the video. He was soon befriended by Ann Marie's circle of friends. When Robert was later introduced to Ann Marie, he fell in love with her. 'We walked up Mount Krisevac together barefoot and did the Stations of the Cross. We prayed for her brother and I also found myself praying: "Dear Lord, if it's your will, give me a small part to play in the evangelization of the world".' His prayer heralded the beginning of a dramatic conversion experience. Robert attended a talk given by Vicka, one of the six Medjugorje visionaries, who claim to have had apparitions of the Virgin Mary. 'I asked her what young people should do to spread the gospel and if, for example, they should give up their jobs. She replied that Our Lady asks us to put God first.'

Robert met Ernest Williams, the founder of Youth 2000, who would also become a key figure in his life. The next day Ernest, a young businessman from Kenilworth, Warwickshire, asked Robert to help film the visionaries during the apparitions. 'I felt really nervous and I kept praying: "Please convert me, please convert me". Then all of a sudden I went to a different place. I saw Christ undergoing his Passion, going up the hill of Calvary and being spat at. Yet his face was full of divine peace and serenity. As he got further and further up Golgotha, I realized that I was following him but I wasn't part of the crowd that was hurting him. He was hauled up on to the cross, but this feeling of hatred, scorn and evil was surrounding him. After he eventually died, the sadness I felt turned to anger and then to rage. I remember saying: "These people have killed my Jesus". Then I suddenly realized that these people were my sins. All that anger and rage poured in on me, and I felt a deep repentance. I saw what I had done and what I'd failed to do. Then I opened my eyes, and the visionaries walked towards me. I felt like Our Lady was asking me to let go of Ann Marie, to let her die. I was saying: "No, no". In the end I said "Yes". Then I felt an intense physical pain like a sword going through my chest and then the sensation of a healing balm.

'The next day I went to pray outside Vicka's house because she had been instrumental in helping me to take Our Lady's messages seriously. I saw Our Lady bless Ernest three times. Then I saw a black flaming cross against a red background.'

Soon afterwards Robert discovered that the same scene is said to occur when the Virgin Mary leaves the Medjugorje visionaries after an apparition. It wasn't until a few years later, after much prayer and reflection, that the full meaning of Robert's own vision of Calvary gradually enfolded. He began to realize that Mary herself would have witnessed exactly the same event, as her son Jesus carried the cross.

The next day, Robert left Medjugorje. On the coach journey to Split he met a young Croatian man of the same age. After he prayed the joyful, sorrowful and glorious mysteries of the rosary, Robert felt compelled to ask the young stranger to pray with him. He gave him a prayer book in Croatian that he had picked up in Medjugorje. It turned out that his travelling companion had always been drawn to the Christian faith. As someone living in a Communist country, he had not been able to pursue his interest any further.

Once he returned home, Robert felt a great urgency to live
out the messages of Medjugorje. He attended daily Mass,
prayed the entire rosary, fasted on Wednesdays and Fridays
and read the Bible. Many of his friends, including some at the
university Catholic chaplaincy, thought he had gone mad. An
injury meant he had to stop rowing and he also gave up
playing in the orchestra. He started the Medjugorje Society in
Cambridge and spent three days at the freshers' fair handing
out leaflets. He set up a rosary group which is still going to
this day. He also attended a number of other prayer groups,
including a charismatic one where he was baptized in the
Spirit. 'In short, my faith became my life', he says. 'I needed
to pray and I wanted to pray. I desperately wanted to bring this
message to everyone I met because it had such a dramatic
effect on my life. I felt utterly loved by Jesus and secure in this
knowledge. I knew that he brings new life to all who meet
him.'

His experience in Medjugorje had awakened his faith in a
way he had never previously believed possible. He organized
lectures on Medjugorje and brought in keynote speakers from
all over the world, including Wayne Weibel, an American
Lutheran who became a Catholic and gave up his career as a
journalist to spread the Medjugorje messages; Father Michael
O'Carroll, an accomplished Irish author and Mariologist; and
Father Slavko Barbaric, the spiritual director of the

Medjugorje visionaries. On one occasion, he packed the Cambridge Union with hundreds of students. 'Life was hectic but incredibly fulfilling', he says. 'I felt like I was helping people to find the living God'.

During that year, Robert didn't see Ann Marie, who was now back in Ireland, but they kept in touch by telephone and letter. 'Ann Marie then got a nursing place in Epsom, Surrey, and when she came over we started to go out with each other', recalls Robert. 'I introduced her to my friends, and everyone loved her. At that time, I didn't really understand the extent of what Our Lady had asked me to do by letting go of her. Ann Marie was full of faith and fun and used to make everyone, including me, laugh a lot. I hope that I helped fill in some small way the void which the death of her brother left.' Robert and Ann Marie parted company the following year after Robert's graduation. 'I felt that I might have a vocation to the priesthood so I wanted to discern that'. Robert later discovered that he did not have a vocation. By this time, he had fallen in love with another beautiful young woman, Amanda Godwin.

Robert first met Amanda in Medjugorje on Mount Krisevac, the Hill of the Cross, in 1989. He was helping Ernest Williams, whom he had met the previous summer, to organize the first Youth 2000 international prayer festival in

Medjugorje. Amanda, like Robert, had been touched by Medjugorje, and found encouragement and support through friends they had made there. Robert and Amanda began working with two other young people, Jonathan Stevens and Jane Potvin. They all came together under the banner of Youth 2000 and started to organize retreats for young people.

By now, Robert was in his final year at university. He invited Father Slavko on a tour of Britain. Robert organized talks in Oxford, Cambridge, London, Manchester, Ampleforth and Scotland. He laughs: 'An example of my madness at that time was having to explain to my university supervisor that I would be away for two weeks before my finals because I was driving a priest around the UK. The supervisor was scratching his head in disbelief, but I had a lot of nuns praying for me.' Robert felt strongly that Father Slavko, who died in November 2000 as he led the Stations of the Cross in Medjugorje, would speak to the hearts of young people. The Franciscan friar and parish priest of Medjugorje baptized Robert and Amanda's third daughter, Chiara, at Youth 2000's annual prayer festival in Walsingham in 1999. Ann Marie is Chiara's godmother. 'Father Slavko was very practical and deeply spiritual', recalls Robert. 'My spirituality has its real roots in his incredible, amazing grasp of what it is to be a child of God and Mary'. He was also instrumental in Amanda's conversion. Amanda had abandoned her faith at university, but the priest's words and spiritual books helped to bring her back to the Catholic Church.

Father Slavko was a trained psychotherapist and was called in by the Bishop of Mostar to investigate the alleged visionaries – Mirjana, Ivanka, Ivan, Vicka, Marija and Jacov – shortly after the phenomenon began in 1981. All six received spiritual direction from Father Slavko. He encouraged Eucharistic adoration and prayer before the cross as a source of healing, and promoted the idea of praying from the heart. At one point he invited drug addicts from central Liverpool to live in his house. During Youth 2000's summer festival in 1990, the Franciscan was called out in the middle of the night to mend a leaking prayer tent. He pulled on the first thing he could find and turned up wearing brown trousers that were too short for him and a T-shirt with a picture of Snoopy windsurfing. 'He guided people to the richness of what the Church has to offer through adoration, confession and praying with Our Lady', says Robert. 'He was an inspiration because he had a lot of humour and was very down to earth'.

When he graduated in 1990, Robert took a year out to live in community and work for Youth 2000. He spent the first six months with the Krisevac Community in Dalmally, Scotland. At this time he was still wondering if he had a vocation to the priesthood. Amanda had also taken time out to work full time

143

in active evangelization for Youth 2000. With Jonathan and Jane, Amanda visited schools, university chaplaincies and parishes throughout the country, inviting young people to Youth 2000 retreats. Only ten people turned up to the first retreat in Beckenham, Kent. When 150 came to the second one at the end of 1990, Robert and Amanda knew that God was at work. Their joint commitment to evangelization brought them even closer together. 'Amanda and I had known each other for quite a long time', explains Robert. 'We got to know each other as friends and prayed together'.

In 1991, they were involved in a road accident together in Scotland. The event marked a turning point in their relationship as their friendship blossomed into love. Robert recalls: 'We hit black ice and skidded down a railway embankment. The car turned over on to its roof. The crash had a profound effect on me. At that time I had been going through a tough time with my faith. I was going through a dry period of confusion and doubt, a dark night of the soul, after the initial joy of having met Jesus in a profound way in Medjugorje.'

The following year Robert trained as a barrister in London. Amanda took a job as a researcher for BBC religion. In 1994, Robert and Amanda married and moved to Leeds where Robert began his career as a barrister. Amanda gave up work to embrace full-time motherhood. The couple now have four children – Max, Emmanuelle, Chiara and Maria.

Robert became national director of Youth 2000 in 1997. It was sometimes a struggle trying to balance the demands of Robert's job and family life with his commitment to Youth 2000. He could not have sustained a leadership role without his wife's support. 'Amanda has helped to guide Youth 2000', he says. 'Her input has been key. She's astute, practical and balanced. Since she became a mother and devoted herself to caring for our children, her role has been hidden.'

Robert and Amanda moved out of Leeds to the Yorkshire village of East Keswick on 31 January 1999, the feast of St John Bosco, the patron saint of young people. At first, retreats were organized from an office in their home. The following year Youth 2000 found new premises within the village and in 2003 opened a new school of evangelization to form young missionaries to evangelize in Britain. Several bishops in England and Wales have also given Youth 2000 their blessing. In 1999, the organization was invited by Archbishop Patrick Kelly of Liverpool to lead a celebration in the city's metropolitan cathedral to mark the new millennium.

'It was a high point, although things went wrong', says Robert. A live link to the Vatican was pulled at the last minute.

But as the clock struck midnight, one of the priests present went up to the altar to give a blessing. There was complete and utter silence, and then fireworks started going off outside. Young people went up to the sanctuary to praise God. It was a wonderful, free celebration. Youth 2000 has been peppered with experiences like this.'

There have been hard times too. At one point, Youth 2000 was £100,000 in debt. At times like this Robert has trusted completely in God's providence. He found that the more impossible the situation seemed, the more the donations flowed in. At the end of 2003, he faced another crisis when the venue for the New Year retreat became unavailable at the last minute. With only days to go, he managed to find another venue and contact hundreds of people who had booked on to the retreat. 'It reminds me of the passage from St Paul (2 Corinthians 4:8-9) where "we are subjected to every kind of hardship, but never distressed; we see no way out but we never despair; we are pursued but never cut off; knocked down, but we still have some life in us".'

The same philosophy has underpinned his professional life as a barrister over the last ten years. The work has been demanding and stressful. He has also faced the pressure of knowing that many of his clients would face financial ruin if their case was lost. 'I always prayed that God would give me the work he wanted me to do. I looked at each case as a gift from God.'

On 25 March 2004, the feast of the Annunciation, Robert helped to launch Xt3.com, an on-line Christian record label. The venture was launched jointly with his older brother, John, who used to be the manager of the singer and actress Martine McCutcheon. Xt3 offers young people a forum for expression through music and the arts based on the values of Christianity.

'We want to tell young people that they are a beloved son or daughter of God', says Robert. 'We're not going to change someone's life by piling on the theological truths but we are going to change it by helping them to realize they are Jesus' friend'.